GROWING

IN

GOD

Peggy,

I never intended to write a book like this... "but God" had a different plan. May He use it to grow you more and more into His likeness.
Phil 2:12-13

    With Love In Christ,

    David Goedling

GROWING IN GOD

THE SANCTIFICATION OF THE BELIEVER

DAVID GOODLING

Growing In God
Copyright © 2023 by David Goodling
Contact: GIGYourSanctification@gmail.com

All rights reserved. No part of this book may be reproduced, scanned, transmitted, or utilized in any form, digital or printed without written permission of the author.

Unless otherwise noted, scripture verses are from the YouVersion App., English Standard Version (ESV), 2016.
ISBN: 9798378485260

Internal title page image design & and encouragement by Lauren Goodling
Cover design by David & Vickie Goodling
Cover photo by istockphoto.com, Valle del Lago, Somiedo Nature Park, Asturias, Spain
Back cover photo by istockphoto.com, Silhouette of helping hand Between two climbers
Editorial work performed by Reedsy, Kristen O'Neal

With Loving Dedication:

To my Savior & Lord Jesus Christ

To my wife, Vickie, the most sanctified person I know; for her love, support and help in the years that it took to make *Growing In God* a reality

CONTENTS

FORWARD

PREFACE

CHAPTER 1: INTRODUCTION

CHAPTER 2: EXAMINING OUR BELIEFS IN CHRIST

CHAPTER 3: AM I REALLY SAVED

CHAPTER 4: OUR MANDATE: WHY WE NEED TO GROW

CHAPTER 5: THE BIBLE: GOD'S WORD

CHAPTER 6: THE TRINITY: FATHER, SON AND HOLY SPIRIT

CHAPTER 7: WALK IN THE SPIRIT

CHAPTER 8: KEYS TO WALKING IN THE SPIRIT

CHAPTER 9: MOTIVATION AND COMMITMENT

CHAPTER 10: DISCIPLESHIP

CHAPTER 11: HOLINESS

CHAPTER 12: SIN

CHAPTER 13: GROWING IN GOD

CHAPTER 14: MEASURING OUR GROWTH

CHAPTER 15 – SUMMARY

EPILOGUE

FORWARD

During the course of my twenty-eight years as a teaching Elder in a local church, I have read countless books and blogs on discipleship. While there are certainly some good resources available, there are more that I would hate for someone to pick up. Today's church culture has made discipleship a complicated program or elaborate system of classes, curriculum, leadership skills and relationship building, just to name a few. This emphasis on our knowledge and ability is humorous considering the reminder of **1st Corinthians 1:26-30**, that the people of God are not called based on intellect, creativity or any other positive characteristic. The family of God is made up of a variety of people with differing abilities, but not even one of us is excluded from carrying out the Great Commission. When it comes to discipleship, God kept the plan simple for us and it is most easily stated as, "find someone who is ahead of you spiritually and someone who is behind you spiritually, then get between them and grow together." It is in these small groups and intimate relationships that a supplemental material such as **Growing In God** can help guide discussion and provide starting points for further development. David does a fantastic job as he writes to you, as a new believer, to make you feel as if he has pulled up a chair and is sharing his heart with you. He shares from Scripture how you can grow in your relationship with the one true God. As you walk through this book you have passage after passage from the Word of God that gives clarity to every point he is making, but all the while sharing his personal story and struggles that have aided in his spiritual maturity.

I am honored to recommend this book to you, not only because the content will provide guidance and insight for your spiritual growth, but also because I know David Goodling. I have had the honor of being his Pastor for well over a decade and the opportunity to observe him in the one place most conducive for discipleship…the local church. This is the key place in which God intends for deep discipleship to occur and David has lived this out with so many of our men. This book, written from the heart of a disciple with a desire to make disciples, is a valuable asset to your library. I pray you use it the way I know David intends for it to be used, to grow you up into maturity and enjoy the blessings of being in the Kingdom of God. Information is taught, but passion like David's for the Kingdom is caught. I trust that as you read the information it will strengthen your walk, but more importantly, your passion will be ignited as you share it with others and see them begin growing in Christ.

Pastor Chad Everson

PREFACE

I struggled somewhat with what to include in this section of the book. In the final analysis, I felt that it might make the most sense to include some background and perspective on my own spiritual history, leading into some introductory comments on growing in God.

    I did not come to saving faith in Christ until the age of 43 (as of this writing, I am in my mid-seventies). I was raised in a small town in Western New York. As a young boy, my first religious experience began in a small Presbyterian church in a nearby town. From my earliest memory my mother attended church there. My "Grammy," my mom's mother, lived with us and was always praying and reading her Bible. But for whatever reason, she did not go to church. My mother would drive my sister and me to Sunday School, then go home and return later in time for the church service. My sister and I would attend the service as well, and at its completion, we would all return home. My dad, on the other hand, chose this day to work in the family garden or on some other household project that needed his attention.

This weekly ritual went on into my parents' retirement, until my mom passed in her late sixties. Dad, as far as I remember, never attended church until after my mom died. We never talked about it, so this remains kind of a mystery to me to this day. There is no doubt that my parents loved us, but we never really experienced much communication, a close relationship, or discipline from them. At some point, church became our own choice. By the time I reached high school, I chose – and church was no longer a part of my life.

As I grew into adulthood, I felt that God and religion were for weak people who needed a crutch to help or get them through life. I wasn't one of them. There is a lot more detail in all this, but overall, I lived a very selfish, self-centered life. I thought I was a "good person," but based wholly on my own moral standards. I was married at an early age, had two beautiful children, and divorced after 18 years. Shortly after the divorce, my employer transferred me to Chicago. Though I had experienced some very hard and difficult times during this part of my life, this became a new start for me. My son moved to Chicago with me, and I became a single parent. I was very content in my life despite all that had occurred. I wasn't down or depressed or anything like that. I wasn't searching for something to get me through life; I was fine on my own. But God had a different plan. He revealed Himself to me in an incredible way, and I came to know Him as Savior and Lord. A supernatural God made Himself real to me through natural events. He

PREFACE

used a distant, newly built church steeple at the very beginning of my move to Chicago, and months later, a desire to think and talk about God. Not a particular religion God, just God. After that He used a new administrative assistant, a work supervisor, and the church attached to that steeple to bring my life to Him. There is much more detail to all of this, but the most amazing thing that occurred was probably when I was leaving that church for the first time. As I walked down the sidewalk to my vehicle, I felt compelled to look back at the church. When I did, I was overwhelmed by a sense of leaving my home. At the time, this was very weird and confusing; later, I realized that this was God's way of showing me the desire He had for my life.

After almost 32 years, I am still amazed at what He did and continues to do. He gave me a new life, He gave me a new wife, and no matter what happens in this world, I will live with Him for all eternity. Christ is the real deal, and if you want to find out what that means, all you must do is read His Word, the Bible, which is the source of all knowledge, wisdom, and understanding. There are a lot of false belief systems in this world and many false religions. If you want to know where you came from, why you are here, how to live your life, and what happens when you die, all you must do is go to His Word and read.

Looking back, especially to the latter part of 1990, one of the last things I thought I would ever do was write a book about growing in relationship with the

God of the Bible. At that time, I hadn't even rationalized His reality in my own life. As I said, I thought that God was a crutch that weak people needed or used to get them through life. Whatever He was, or may have been, was of no interest to me. I knew next to nothing about Him; He had no relevance in my life. As I have already stated, that could have been the end of the story... *but God.*

What had happened to me? As time passed, I learned, through the Bible, that God had supernaturally changed my heart. As Titus puts it, "for we ourselves were once foolish, disobedient, led astray, slaves to various passions and pleasures, passing our days in malice and envy, hated by others and hating one another. But when the goodness and loving kindness of God our Savior appeared, he saved us, not because of works done by us in righteousness, but according to his own mercy, by the washing of regeneration and renewal of the Holy Spirit, whom he poured out on us richly through Jesus Christ our Savior, so that being justified by his grace we might become heirs according to the hope of eternal life." (Titus 3:3-7 ESV)

This is true and faithful, not because it happened to me subjectively, but because the Bible proclaims it, objectively. It is God's ancient and reliable truth.

God had "washed, regenerated and renewed" my life. From that time forward, it has been a continual process of my head catching up with my heart. God had changed me, but there was so much I didn't understand that I needed to learn. That is what this book is all about. If you have been changed by the power of the Holy Spirit, you need to continue to grow so that your mind can catch up with what God has done in your heart. He commands it, "Be holy as I am holy!".

Growing In God is, essentially, a book about understanding the need, responsibility, and process for growing in our Christian faith. This all begins by affirming our belief and faith in Christ and understanding the critical role that God's Word plays as the primary and key resource in all that we are about to undertake. We must then understand the elements and processes God uses to grow us, the roles of the Trinity (especially of the Holy Spirit), and finally the practical aspects of what we need to do in our daily lives to grow – and how we can measure that growth.

Though I have written about several different subjects in this book, I truly believe God's overall purpose is to help believers grow in their faith and their relationship with Him. Please read the book slowly and carefully. Read and meditate on all the scripture references: they are the true source of anything that would be of value to you. I hope you end up amazed at what only He can do.

If you are already a believer, it is my prayer that you will use this material to learn to love and honor God more than you ever thought possible. If you somehow come across this book and you are not a believer, I pray that you will open yourself up to a fair and objective study of the evidence that supports His reality. In that regard, I would recommend the book or movie entitled *The Case for Christ*.[1]

Regardless of where you fall, May the Holy Spirit lead your way.

Situated at the bottom of the mountain, we had just moved in, and our new surroundings were comfortable, secure, and stable. Our previous dwelling had been dark, cold, and uncomfortable, though we had not realized it at the time. For most of our lives, it had felt normal. We had been secure in our routine – we were doing what we felt was right and what we had been conditioned to. We had not realized how wrong we had been. What we were experiencing now was in such drastic contrast to the old way of life. We thought we had lived in the light, but it seemed pale and dirty compared to where we were now...

CHAPTER ONE

INTRODUCTION

If we claim to be true Christians, the single most important thing in our lives should be to grow in our relationship with God. If we think back to when we first realized our faith in Christ, we had no real understanding of the Bible, who God was, how He functions in the life of a believer, or our responsibility to find all of these things out. We were all at the bottom of a very large mountain called Sanctification that we needed to ascend – and for the most part, were left on our own to figure out how to do this. We had not been taught how to get involved in real spiritual growth. We did not understand our need to begin the process of our sanctification: becoming set apart, growing, and holy in our Christian faith. We had begun the ascent, but our progress was slow and labored.

Often, after years of this, we remain near the bottom of the mountain, looking up and wondering why we have doubts about our belief. We find it hard to apply our faith to the difficulties that life brings. As a result, we tend to live in defeat instead of in the victory of our Savior, Jesus Christ.

I have been a Christian for over 30 years, and though I have grown in my faith in that period, my overall spiritual growth is, at best, anemic and severely deficient. For though I have the Spirit of God established in me, I have not fed it adequately over these many years. Though I will take full blame for this, the church has been lacking as well. It has not always set its people on a path of understanding or accountability or modeled the growth we should be expected to attain and achieve. The typical new believer comes to faith, the church shouts *Hallelujah*, and so begins a life of weekly church attendance, Sunday school, fellowship, and for some, service. It's like we choose an occupation to pursue in life – say finance, medicine, accounting, or yes, even rocket science – skip school, and go right to work. Why learn all the foundational, fundamental, and essential basics of the job? We'll figure it out as we go! In the real world, this will not work, but we allow it in the most important position of our whole lives: being a follower of the Lord Jesus Christ. We end up more involved in our religion then in our relationship with God.

It seems that from the very beginning, God put a desire in my heart to meet with other Christian men, one on one or in small groups – not so much for social reasons, but to grow in our faith and walk with the Lord. We had fellowship, we studied the Bible, and we had

INTRODUCTION

many spiritual discussions. At that time, *discipleship* was not a word that I really knew, used, or understood. I just sensed a need in myself and in others to go deeper and discover more about this God we had committed our lives to. We also found a common bond in many difficult life issues, and we looked to God and to each other to try and understand them and find healing in our lives.

After all these years, it is only now that I have come to the realization of how important and critical it is to understand and be educated in the foundational and fundamental principles of growing in God's Word.

It is the goal of this book to try and communicate some of the essential information that we need to know and understand in order to provide a basis for growing in God and in His Word (our sanctification). Though many topics are presented and covered separately, they all fit together and help us see the process we must follow to pursue our relationship with God and help it flourish. So, with all that said, let's pray God's Word from Ephesians.

> We pray: "that the God of our Lord Jesus Christ, the Father of glory, may give you the Spirit of wisdom and of revelation in the knowledge of him, having the eyes of your hearts enlightened, that you may know what is the hope to which he has called you, what are the riches of his glorious inheritance in the saints, and what is the

immeasurable greatness of his power toward us who believe, according to the working of his great might." (Ephesians 1:17-19 ESV)

We pray this now in the mighty name of our Lord and Savior Jesus Christ. Amen!

CHAPTER TWO

EXAMINING OUR BELIEF IN CHRIST

As I said in the preface, God used some amazing things in my life to reveal the truth of His reality and change my heart and mind about what and who He is. That was basically my conversion experience. It wasn't about what man could say or do. It was about the power of the living God. I love what Ephesians says about this in chapter 2:

> "For by grace you have been saved through faith. And this is not your own doing; it is the gift of God, not a result of works, so that no one may boast." (Ephesians 2:8-9 ESV)

We, or others, can convince our minds of many things, but only God changes the heart and the essence of who we are. That's what He did to me.

If you've professed Christ and claim to be a Christian, you should have at least, a basic understanding of what that means (i.e., committing your life to Jesus Christ as Savior and Lord). We will talk more about this as we go, but for now, let's consider some of the main points of what drew us to Christianity, or convinced us, at least intellectually, to join this faith.

Perhaps you have always considered yourself a Christian: you come from a Christian home, or someone asked you, *if you died today, would you go to heaven or hell?* and hell was an option you didn't want left on the table. There are many ways you might describe how you came to faith or how someone talked you into it, but let's consider something more universally personal.

Where did I come from? Why am I here? What happens when I die?

To begin this section, I decided to look up sayings and quotes about what *life* is. As you can imagine, there was a rather large diversity of comments and thoughts on this word. Some were short, simple and to the point. Others were deep, thoughtful, or philosophical. Most had a more secular viewpoint, while some ventured out into the Divine.

It is probably fair to say that *life* involves some level of the active participation of an individual from birth to death. We can look at it from the past, the present, and the future. In one sense, it has been completed; in another, it is in process; and lastly, it is only to be thought about or anticipated. Though it can be happy and joyful, it can also be frustrating, difficult, and confusing. It is active and real. It is talked about, discussed, debated – even though, for the most part, it is in full view of everyone. I guess we all have an opinion about what life should be and how it should be conducted.

Ultimately, though, I think *life* revolves around the three questions of this section. *Where did I come from? Why am I here?* and *What happens when I die?*

These can be haunting questions. They may be openly discussed and debated with strong opinions and conclusions in the public square, but in the private and secluded thoughts of our minds, they remain an enigma. Perhaps these three questions, or a form of them, are what life has you asking right now, and what brought you to the Christian Faith. They are important questions to consider as you think about your commitment to Christ and as you begin to learn and grow in your faith.

Why And How Are We Saved

The Bible tells us that the sin of Adam and Eve was passed down to all of us: "Therefore, just as sin came into the world through one man, and death through sin, and so death spread to all men because all sinned—" (Romans 5:12 ESV). This sin that was passed down to all of us has severed our spiritual relationship with God. The Bible tells us that we are dead (spiritually) in our sins. Salvation (being saved) is how that relationship is restored. But why are we saved? Why did God provide a way to repair, restore and redeem us?

To begin with, there is nothing in us, nothing we can say or do, no goodness or talent or skill we have, that can bring us into favor with God. It is only by His mercy and grace. This is what Romans says about who we are before God saves us:

> "as it is written: "None is righteous, no, not one; no one understands; no one seeks for God. All have turned aside; together they have become worthless; no one does good, not even one."
> "Their throat is an open grave; they use their tongues to deceive."
> "The venom of asps is under their lips."
> "Their mouth is full of curses and bitterness."
> "Their feet are swift to shed blood; in their paths are ruin and misery, and the way of peace they have not known."
> "There is no fear of God before their eyes.""
> (Romans 3:10-18 ESV)

As we have already stated, spiritually, we are all dead in our sins and trespasses and without hope. So why does God save anyone? He saves for the same reason He created, as Charles Spurgeon put it: for His "glory, honor, and pleasure,".[1] He continues:

> "No other answer can be consistent with reason. Whatever other replies men may propound, no other can be really sound. If they will for one moment consider that there was a time when God had no creatures—when he dwelt alone, the mighty maker of ages, glorious in an uncreated solitude, divine in his eternal loneliness—"I am and there is none beside me"—can any one answer this question—Why did God make creatures to exist?—in any other way than by answering it thus: "He made them for his own pleasure and for his own glory."[1]

Again, He saves for the same reason. In Revelation, the Elders acknowledged God and cast their crowns before the throne and said:

> "Worthy are you, our Lord and God, to receive glory and honor and power, for you created all things, and by your will they existed and were created." (Revelation 4:11 ESV)

The next part of the question is, *how does God save?*

Simply speaking, God saves by His mercy and grace, by grace alone, through faith alone. He sent His one and only Son to die on a cross as our substitute, imputing our sin to Himself and His righteousness to those who believe. As a result of our election, God calls us, regenerates our hearts, and gives us faith and belief to trust in Christ. Our acts, thoughts, and attitudes against God become apparent, and we respond by turning away from them and repenting of our sin. We are now alive in Christ. The gap in our relationship with God is eliminated, and we are reconciled with God through His Son. Jesus has become our Savior and Lord.

If you believe these things, then in all likelihood you have received salvation in Christ and can be considered a Christian. But how do I know for sure?

CHAPTER THREE

AM I REALLY SAVED?

In 1 John 5:13, God's Word tells us that if we "believe in the name of the Son of God, that you may know that you have eternal life." However, as we live out our lives in Christ, we may experience doubts or situations that challenge the reality or conviction of our faith. There may be times when we wonder why we don't always "feel" or live out our beliefs in a sincere or committed way. This verse also relies on the true reality of our conversion. To help us in this dilemma and to sort out our concerns, God's Word once again informs us that there are certain things in our lives that are indicators of true salvation. In 2 Corinthians 13:5 (ESV), Paul tells us to test ourselves: "Examine yourselves, to see whether you are in the faith. Test yourselves. Or do you not realize this about yourselves, that Jesus Christ is in you?—unless indeed you fail to meet the test!"

At this point, it is important to re-emphasize some things about having faith in Christ. First of all, there is absolutely nothing you can do to earn, increase, diminish or otherwise affect your standing before God in Christ. Once saved, God only sees you through the righteousness of His Son. In that sense, you are perfect and holy in His sight. "Therefore, if anyone is in Christ, he is a new creation. The old has passed away; behold, the new has come." (2 Corinthians 5:17 ESV)

We have what is called *positional sanctification*. This means that at the point we are saved – born again as a new creation – God sees us in a "position" of righteousness because He looks at us through the righteousness of His Son. We have been saved for all eternity.

Secondly, though we are secure in Him for all eternity, we still need to learn, grow, understand, and act out this new relationship we have with God – this is called *ongoing sanctification*. We still live in the flesh of the old man; we must learn to kill that flesh and become more like Christ, the object of our discipleship.

> "And those who belong to Christ Jesus have crucified the flesh with its passions and desires." (Galatians 5:24 ESV)
> "But I say, walk by the Spirit, and you will not gratify the desires of the flesh." (Galatians 5:16 ESV)
> "For if you live according to the flesh you will die, but if by the Spirit you put to death the deeds of the body, you will live." (Romans 8:13 ESV)

To be obedient to these verses, we need both *ongoing* and *continual* sanctification. We will be defining and talking more about this as we go.

So how do we examine ourselves? What things do we need to consider to help validate our conversion and belief in Christ? As the old saying goes, if we were accused of being a Christian, would there be enough evidence to convict us?

Do our opinions, attitudes, motives, and actions line up with God's Word? Though there are many detailed and scripturally supported issues we could look at, the bottom line is this: a true believer displays an initially and ongoing changed life. They actively pursue righteousness. John MacArthur does an excellent job at enumerating and discussing some of these in an article entitled "Examine Yourself".[1] Below are some of the sub-titles of this article along with a short synopsis of each:

The Distinguishing Mark of a Christian[2]

The Bible tells us that "all our righteous acts are like filthy rags" before the Lord (Isaiah 64:6 NIV). This section helps us understand more emphatically, that our salvation – our righteous standing before God – is not based on our good works or righteous acts but solely on the righteousness of Christ. If we are truly saved, our lives should reflect an ongoing and continual pursuit of this righteousness. It should be in ongoing humility of this fact that we are to lead our lives, constantly striving to be like Him.

A Distinct Testimony[3]

The story of how we came to faith in Christ is our *personal testimony*. This testimony should be evident to others as we lead our lives in this world. Do we just do as others do by blending in and hiding our light under a bushel basket? Or do we reflect the light of Christ to those around us. People should see a difference in who we are, what we do, and what we say. Our whole lives should be a testimony to Christ.

An Obedient Life[4]

In this section, MacArthur states that "a child of God is characterized by obedience."[5] The law of God has been fulfilled in Christ and is to be followed and obeyed in our lives as believers. There is really no such thing as salvation without submission. When God saves us and we become followers of Christ, we are to treat Christ as both savior and Lord. As our Savior, He has given us forgiveness and redeemed us from our sins. As our Lord, He asks us to be obedient and follow all of His statutes, rules and commandments. The mark of a true Christian is an obedient life.

Sincere Worship[6]

Here, MacArthur admonishes us to have honest, heartfelt, and sincere motives and desires to glorify God in all that we are and do and to show true gratitude and thankfulness for who God is and what He has done.

> "I appeal to you therefore, brothers, by the mercies of God, to present your bodies as a living sacrifice, holy and acceptable to God, which is your spiritual worship." (Romans 12:1 ESV)
>
> "Therefore, let us be grateful for receiving a kingdom that cannot be shaken, and thus let us offer to God acceptable worship, with reverence and awe," (Hebrews 12:28 ESV)

A Biblical Perspective of Money and Materialism[7]

A true believer understands that the only valuable thing in this life is the faith and belief we have in God through Christ. Money and materialism should not be the focus or priority of a believer's life. The Bible tells us that we cannot serve two masters. We will either hate the one and love the other or be devoted to the one and despise the other. You cannot serve both God and money (Matthew 6:24).

An Uncritical Love of Others[8]

True believers strive to have relationships based on non-judgmental attitudes (Matthew 7:1) and look inwardly before judging someone else (Matthew 7:3-5). The primary concern of a true believer should be the welfare of others, looking to do to others as others would do to them (Matthew 7:12). They strive to obey the second greatest commandment: to "love your neighbor as yourself" (Matthew 22:39 NIV). This includes your enemies and those that would come against you.

A Deceptive Illusion of Eternal Life[9]

In this section, MacArthur points out the delusion some people have in thinking that the road that leads to eternal life is broad. Some people think they can accept Christ as Savior and then live in a worldly and self-righteous manner. Matthew 7:21 (NIV) sums up the result of this deception: "Not everyone who says to me, 'Lord, Lord,' will enter the kingdom of heaven, but only the one who does the will of my Father who is in heaven."

It is important to note, however, that a true believer is never perfect in being a Christian – they are always striving to attain it. Our desire and motivation is to please God and represent His Son well: to bring glory and honor to His name.

When we are saved, the Holy Spirit takes up residence in our lives. The process of sanctification begins as we start a new life and begin to shed the grave cloths of the old man of sin. It is the Spirit that convicts us of sin and inspires us to live holy and righteous lives. If we aspire to righteousness, it will be borne out in how we live our lives. We should begin to produce the fruit of the Spirit. Here are some things to consider as we examine ourselves.

God sets the rules and standards for moral living

From the very beginning, God made it clear and unambiguous what the moral standard for mankind should be. We find the foundation of His righteous law in the Ten Commandments (Deuteronomy 5:7-21). In order to have an objective standard, our laws and rules must come from a power outside of mankind – a power that transcends our subjective opinion and preferences. Otherwise, we are left with relative morality: an *if it feels good, do it* type of mentality. Who then is right? If some universal law is desired, it will be determined and enforced by the person or group with the most power and influence. The powers of our world become dictatorial and self-serving, and as a result, our world becomes chaotic and out of control. There is no objective standard of right and wrong. The creator of the universe and His rules become meaningless.

Ongoing sin, conviction, and repentance

> "If we say we have no sin, we deceive ourselves, and the truth is not in us. If we confess our sins, he is faithful and just to forgive us our sins and to cleanse us from all unrighteousness." (1 John 1:8-9 ESV)

These verses tell us that even after we become Christians, we continue to sin. But true believers are convicted and burdened by their sin. They desire to acknowledge it, repent, and seek forgiveness and reconciliation with God and man. To *repent* means to "feel or express sincere regret or remorse for one's wrongdoing or sin."[10] It means turning from sin to move in a righteous direction – a direction that would honor and glorify God.

The Spirit bears witness to true faith

> "The Spirit himself bears witness with our spirit that we are children of God," (Romans 8:16 ESV)

As we have already established, God's grace saves us from our sins. He does this by regenerating our hearts and making us new creatures in Christ Jesus. We were dead in our trespasses and sins, but we are now made alive in Christ. We are born again! When this happens, the Holy Spirit of God resides in us. The Spirit bears witness to this fact by producing godly characteristics and attributes in us, which the Bible calls *the fruit of the Spirit*. Galatians 5:22-24 (ESV) tells us: "But the fruit of the Spirit is love, joy, peace, patience, kindness, goodness, faithfulness, gentleness, self-control; against such things there is no law. And those who belong to Christ Jesus have crucified the flesh with its passions and desires."

What we must realize, however, is that the Biblical definition of these fruits is much different than the world's. For example, *love* should always be motivated by our love for God. It is sacrificial, unconditional and giving. *Joy* is not based on our circumstances but our relationship with God and the future we have in His eternal kingdom. (For a more thorough understanding of these fruits, read *The Fruitful Life* by Jerry Bridges.[11])

We can test ourselves against each of these nine fruits to see how we're doing. We will not always be successful at producing these fruits, but it should always be our desire, our motivation, and our conviction. We will remember a time when these fruits were too easily compromised by the flesh and the influence of the world.

The Beatitudes in Matthew 5 also show us the characteristics of a true believer: "poor in spirit," "those who mourn," "those who hunger and thirst for righteousness," "the merciful," "the pure in heart," "the peacemakers." Do these attributes describe your character now that you profess Christ in your life?

If you are disappointed or upset with how well you measure up to these biblical standards, it doesn't necessarily mean you are not a Christian. It may point to the sad fact that as one, you never learned or were taught some of these foundational truths. You got saved but spent little time on serious, internal spiritual growth. In short, you were never really discipled.

Let me end this section with a quote from MacArthur's article:

> "The Bible makes it clear that those who are genuinely saved are righteous and holy. They still sin, but with decreasing frequency. A true believer hates his sin (cf., Rom. 7:15-25) and repents of it, hungering and thirsting for what is right. He obeys God, loves his brother, and hates the evil world system. No one can be a Christian and continue living the way he did before he knew Christ. Making a decision years ago, going to an inquiry room, walking an aisle, or reading a tract on how to accept Christ is not a biblical criterion for salvation—the issue is what your life is like right now. If sin and unrighteousness characterize your life, there is a possibility you are a disobedient Christian—but there is a greater possibility you are not a Christian at all."[12]

A Word About Trust

When it comes to our belief or faith in Christ, we are told to have *trust*. But what does this really mean? Are we to trust in our own logic, rationale, feelings, or emotions? To trust means to be assured, but what are we trusting, and who are we assured in when it comes to our faith? Our trust needs to be objective.

In the BSF (Bible Study Fellowship) tract entitled "Steps to Assurance," it states this about trust:

> "Trust (be assured) that having received Christ into your life, you are sealed with God's Holy Spirit and stamped with God's name on you. You may or may not "feel" different, but you don't need to. Your trust is not based on your feelings but on the authority of the Word of God and His promises to you."[13]
>
> "And it is God who establishes us with you in Christ, and has anointed us, and who has also put his seal on us and given us his Spirit in our hearts as a guarantee." (2 Corinthians 1:21-22 ESV)
>
> "Whoever has the Son has life; whoever does not have the Son of God does not have life. I write these things to you who believe in the name of the Son of God, that you may know that you have eternal life." (1 John 5:12-13 ESV)

What If I Fail the Test?

At this point, if you are questioning or unsure of where you stand, you should seek counsel from a trusted pastor.

If we have established our identity in Christ, we can move forward in learning what the Bible tells us we need to do from this point. As stated earlier, there were some key things that I never comprehended about the responsibility I had to grow in my faith. I believe these things can be of great value to both new and existing believers alike.

CHAPTER FOUR

OUR MANDATE: WHY WE NEED TO GROW

Our overall objective is to glorify God. To achieve this, we need to walk in the Spirit and produce His fruit. And to do *this*, we need to grow in our relationship with God and His Word. Growth relies on our sanctification by the power of the Holy Spirit, which relies on our study of God's Word. Understanding most of this has hopefully been conveyed in the preceding chapters. In this section, let's talk a little more about our mandate and why it's important to grow in God and His Word.

If we are to walk in the Spirit, produce His fruit, and be an effective follower of Jesus Christ, we must grow to maturity in our faith. As Hebrews 5:13-14 (ESV) tells us, "for everyone who lives on milk is unskilled in the word of righteousness, since he is a child. But solid food is for the mature, for those who have their powers of discernment trained by constant practice to distinguish good from evil."

As we have already seen, we need to grow spiritually because God commands it (1 Peter 1:13-16 ESV). As Christians, we should need no other reason. But God does not command this to create undo pressure or discomfort in our lives. He does it for our good. The more we learn and grow, the easier life becomes. Not because our difficulties or life situations improve, but because we learn to place our trust and faith in God and rely on Him. We learn to live in the victory we already have in Christ.

My wife is a wonderful example of this. In November of 2014, she was diagnosed with ocular melanoma. This is a cancer of the eye and is relatively rare, occurring in 6 out of every million people. On the more serious side, it can lead to liver, lung, or other major organ cancers, which have low survival rates. Treatment may still result in eye or vision loss. In her case, it was caught very early, and the treatment option recommended was to sew a radiation plaque on the back of her eye in order to kill the cancerous tumor.

You may be able to imagine the trauma and emotion that this whole ordeal elicited. But there is something else you need to know about my wife. Over many, many decades, she has always been faithful to study and grow in her relationship with God: diligent in her early morning quiet time to study God's Word and pray, faithful to memorize God's Word, and dedicated, over many years, to commit to the rigorous work and

OUR MANDATE: WHY WE NEED TO GROW

study required of the BSF (Bible Study Fellowship) program. She has been faithful to attend church and Sunday school, to love and counsel other women, and to serve in many other capacities. Vickie has been faithful to her God, increasing her faith and trust and realizing that He must be her first refuge and not her last resort. Because of this, and in the midst of all that was happening, her heart was drawn to say, "Wow, only 6 in one million. God has picked me out in a special way to go through this. I can't wait to see what He will do." Could she say this out of her own power and strength, or some special quality she was gifted with? No! She could say this because over these many years, she had taken the time to develop a true, firm, and abiding faith in God. Her assurances were not found in what man could do, but in what God had already done. Vickie knew that God had a plan and would use this for her good and to His glory.

Scripture shows us many examples of this type of faith. We see it lived out in the lives of Noah, Moses, Abraham, Joseph, Jesus, and Paul. We must grow this type of faith in ourselves so we can more easily face the inevitable difficulties that life, in a sin-filled world, will present to us – but more importantly, so we can honor and glorify God and avoid the sin of unbelief and the creation of counterfeit gods. We will be talking more about this as we go.

Our goal and purpose should be to look like the Savior who God sent, who "died for all, that they which live should not henceforth live unto themselves, but unto him which died for them, and rose again." (2 Corinthians 5:15 KJV)

Coming to know Christ as Savior and Lord has changed my whole life. It has changed my whole perspective on why I'm here, what my purpose is, and what the future holds. To be chosen by God, redeemed from my sins by the death of His Son, and given a whole new perspective of life from God's Word, is nothing short of miraculous. But that was over 30 years ago. What has happened since then, and how has my relationship with God grown? How have I changed as a result? There has definitely been increased understanding, but I feel there could have been so much more growth. I'm afraid I've fallen into the same trap that many others have. I've attended church faithfully, done Bible studies, and served in many capacities, but I have neglected my own personal spiritual growth. I am deficient, especially after so many years, in truly knowing God, and in understanding and living out God's Word in my life. John MacArthur said that if we spent as much time on the *inner man* (spiritual) as the *outer man* (physical), it would revolutionize the church.[1] The inner, or spiritual man, tends only to get fed once a week from the church pulpit, and that feeding is based on what the Pastor believes is the need of his flock at a particular time in the life of his church. Though generally applicable, it doesn't necessarily line up with what an individual person really needs to hear, know, take in, and be fed with. It doesn't, and by its nature can't, take into account the individual needs of each person in the congregation. Try feeding the physical man once a week and see how that works out. The frequency and method of feeding the inner man varies from person to person, but I think it's fair to say that we all tend to fall into the situation outlined above. We don't realize enough that this neglect of the spiritual man affects the physical man. This shows up in our vulnerability to temptation and sin, in our neglected relationships, and in our inability to handle difficult and challenging times and situations. Why? Because the spiritual man is weak and anemic and eventually the flesh wins out.

Ongoing spiritual growth is essential to a healthy Christian. We must feed the inner man daily if we are to survive and flourish in this life. It's not optional for us. God commands it: "Therefore, preparing your minds for action, and being sober-minded, set your hope fully on the grace that will be brought to you at the revelation of Jesus Christ. As obedient children, do not be conformed to the passions of your former ignorance, but as he who called you is holy, you also be holy in all your conduct, since it is written, "You shall be holy, for I am holy." (1 Peter 1:13-16 ESV)

So the questions become: how do we become holy? How do we grow to look and act more like the God who saved us? As I mentioned in the introduction, the process God uses to do this is called *sanctification*.

It includes such things as quiet time, prayer, Bible study, church attendance, and service; but the daily reading, meditation, and study of God's Word is of primary and significant importance.

But how does God use His Word to change us? Most of us will follow a reading or study plan or just open the Bible and begin to read. We may never have understood or been taught the process God uses to make His Word effectual in our lives. We need to think about what environment and in what relationships this might best be carried out.

Before we tackle any of this, we must first examine ourselves, affirm our salvation in Christ, evaluate our life in view of His Lordship and our sin, pray, and make a covenant with God to move forward in an effort to grow in our faith, reduce sin in our lives, become more like Christ and do all this to the glory and honor of the Triune God.

CHAPTER FIVE

THE BIBLE: GOD'S WORD

Most Christians will acknowledge the Bible as a main source of knowledge and understanding concerning their faith. Unfortunately, we don't often use it in a significant way to lead our lives and grow in our relationship with God. We tend to rely more on our own will or opinions, or on the will or opinions of others when we make both small and significant life decisions or handle painful, difficult, or challenging situations. As stated before, we tend to feed and rely on the outer man and ignore the inner spiritual man. The Bible has not become a true source of life for us but more like something we take to church, Bible study, or place on our nightstand or coffee table and point to as a symbol of our faith. I cannot emphasize this enough: we need to learn to study God's Word so that it becomes the main source of wisdom and understanding in our lives. We should be *capturing* all things (taking every thought captive) to the obedience of Christ, *evaluating* all things in the light of God's Word, and *collaborating* in prayer and with *godly council* before making decisions or responding to the things that take place in our lives

Capturing all things to the obedience of Christ

> "We destroy arguments and every lofty opinion raised against the knowledge of God, and take every thought captive to obey Christ," (2 Corinthians 10:5 ESV)

Evaluating all things in the light of God's Word

> "Your word is a lamp to my feet and a light to my path." (Psalm 119:105 ESV)

Collaborating in prayer

> "Do not be anxious about anything, but in everything by prayer and supplication with thanksgiving let your requests be made known to God." (Philippians 4:6 ESV)

With Godly counsel:

> "Where there is no guidance, a people falls, but in an abundance of counselors there is safety." (Proverbs 11:14 ESV)

"The way of a fool is right in his own eyes, but a wise man listens to advice." Proverbs 12:15 ESV)

We will talk more about this later, but for now, let's enumerate some of the things we need to remember about God's Word, *through* God's Word.

God's Word is Our Instruction for Living

> "All Scripture is breathed out by God and profitable for teaching, for reproof, for correction, and for training in righteousness, that the man of God may be complete, equipped for every good work." (2 Timothy 3:16-17 ESV)

God's Word is Inerrant

> "Sanctify them in the truth; your word is truth." (John 17:17 ESV)
> "The words of the Lord are pure words, like silver refined in a furnace on the ground, purified seven times." (Psalm 12:6 ESV)

God's Word is Real

> "For the word of God is living and active, sharper than any two-edged sword, piercing to the division of soul and of spirit, of joints and of

marrow, and discerning the thoughts and intentions of the heart." (Hebrews 4:12 ESV)

God's Word is to Be Treasured

"I have not departed from the commandment of his lips; I have treasured the words of his mouth more than my portion of food." (Job 23:12 ESV)

Jesus Is the Word

"In the beginning was the Word, and the Word was with God, and the Word was God. All things were made through him, and without him was not any thing made that was made. In him was life, and the life was the light of men." (John 1:1, 3-4 ESV)

God's Word Is the Law

"The law of the Lord is perfect, reviving the soul; the testimony of the Lord is sure, making wise the simple; the precepts of the Lord are right, rejoicing the heart; the commandment of the Lord is pure, enlightening the eyes; the fear of the Lord is clean, enduring forever; the rules of the Lord are true, and righteous altogether. More to be desired are they than gold, even much fine gold; sweeter also than honey and drippings of the honeycomb. Moreover, by them is your servant warned; in keeping them there is great reward." (Psalm 19:7-11 ESV)

The Word is Life

"It is the Spirit who gives life; the flesh is no help at all. The words that I have spoken to you are spirit and life." (John 6:63 ESV)

The Word is Timeless

"for "All flesh is like grass and all its glory like the flower of grass. The grass withers, and the flower falls, but the word of the Lord remains forever."" (1 Peter 1:24-25a ESV)

The Word is Our Defense and Protection

"Finally, be strong in the Lord and in the strength of his might. Put on the whole armor of God, that you may be able to stand against the schemes of the devil… and take the helmet of salvation, and the sword of the Spirit, which is the word of God," (Ephesians 6:10-11, 17 ESV)

The Word Gives Light, Direction, and Shows Us the Way

> "Your word is a lamp to my feet and a light to my path." (Psalm 119:105 ESV)

CHAPTER SIX

THE TRINITY: FATHER, SON, AND HOLY SPIRIT

There are many factors that we need to consider and learn about if we are going to understand and apply the process God uses to grow and sanctify us in our Christian faith. One of great importance is *the Trinity*: the Father, Son and Holy Spirit. We need to understand how they affect us as they operate as the triune God in their unified yet separate and distinct persons. The role of the Holy Spirit is especially important to the responsibility we have to grow in God.

Nowhere in the Bible do we see the word, *Trinity*. The word came about in an effort to define the nature of God, as seen in Scripture, where the Father, Son, and Holy Spirit are defined as one God yet three persons. To state this a little differently, the three persons of the Trinity are related to each other on an equal basis, but each has a separate role. It is important to note that each member of the Trinity, though they live in complete harmony and unity, is separate and distinct in each of their persons. Jesus was one in relationship with His Father, but He played a separate and distinct role (person) as the Son. God was not one person playing three roles, but three persons unified in one Godhead. It is important that we maintain a correct understanding of this truth. A good example of this can be found in the doctrine of *atonement*, where the Father's wrath is poured out on the Son to achieve redemption, justification and reconciliation for the sinner. In this sense, the Father and the Son must be separate and distinct persons. This may become clearer as we define each person of the Trinity individually.

We even see this concept played out at the beginning of the Bible. In the first verse of Genesis ("In the beginning God...) the Hebrew word for God is "Elohim". Most sources I researched, defined this word in a similar manner:

> "The name commonly used for God in the Old Testament is the Hebrew word *Elohim*. It is also found in the singular form *El* and *Elah*. Whenever we find the English word "God" used in the Old Testament, it is a translation of this Hebrew word *Elohim* or one of its forms.
>
> The exact meaning of *Elohim* is not known though it seems to contain the idea of strength and power.
>
> The noun *Elohim* is plural, but it is always used with a singular verb when it speaks of the true God. This indicates a unity and diversity within

THE TRINITY: FATHER, SON, AND HOLY SPIRIT

the nature of God. This unity and diversity is revealed in Scripture as the doctrine of the Trinity."[1]

Jewish sources define this word in a similar way but do not of course support a reference to the Trinity.

In the New Testament, we see many references that reveal the concept of the Trinity:

> "Go therefore and make disciples of all nations, baptizing them in the name of the Father and of the Son and of the Holy Spirit," (Matthew 28:19 ESV)

> "But the Helper, the Holy Spirit, whom the Father will send in my name (Jesus), he will teach you all things and bring to your remembrance all that I have said to you." (John 14:26 ESV)

> "according to the foreknowledge of God the Father, in the sanctification of the Spirit, for obedience to Jesus Christ and for sprinkling with his blood: May grace and peace be multiplied to you." (1 Peter 1:2 ESV)

Though we will never fully comprehend the meaning of the Trinity, it's important to understand the role and responsibility of each person it represents.

Before we differentiate their roles, let's talk about what the three have in common. First, they are all part of the *Godhead*: one God, three persons. Though they have different and distinct roles, they act as one sovereign, omnipotent, omniscient, omnipresent, immutable, holy God. They were all present at the time of creation:

> "In the beginning, God created the heavens and the earth. The earth was without form and void, and darkness was over the face of the deep. And the Spirit of God was hovering over the face of the waters." (Genesis 1:1-2 ESV)

> "In the beginning was the Word, and the Word was with God, and the Word was God." "And the Word became flesh and dwelt among us, and we have seen his glory, glory as of the only Son from the Father, full of grace and truth." (John 1:1, 14 ESV)

So, in essence, there is no difference in their spiritual nature; their attributes are one and the same. They may have different roles and function differently in relationship to mankind, but in the final analysis, they are one and share all powers of the Godhead. They always act in perfect harmony.

Now let's try and define their individual roles:

THE TRINITY: FATHER, SON, AND HOLY SPIRIT

God The Father

Though all persons of the Trinity display close, loving intimacy, the word "Father" denotes a special relationship that is not used in the title of the other two. God, individually, is probably thought of first and foremost as the "creator God" – mighty and powerful, bringing blessings on those who obey His commandments, and curses on those who don't. "See, I am setting before you today a blessing and a curse: the blessing, if you obey the commandments of the Lord your God, which I command you today, and the curse, if you do not obey the commandments of the Lord your God, but turn aside from the way that I am commanding you today, to go after other gods that you have not known." (Deuteronomy 11:26-28 ESV)

We would also have a sense of the Father's role in planning, leading, and directing the Son and Holy Spirit. But when the word *Father* is used, we more accurately see the role He desires with His people. He is being paternal, seeing us as His children and wanting the very best for us, as any father would. "Every good gift and every perfect gift is from above, coming down from the Father of lights, with whom there is no variation or shadow due to change." (James 1:17 ESV) The best expression of this kind of fatherly love was shown when He sent His only Son to die for our sins. We can be thankful that we serve a loving Father and not an impersonal deity absent from a relationship with his people.

God The Son – Jesus Christ

We know in the book of John that Jesus identifies Himself as God when He says, "Have I been with you so long, and you still do not know me, Philip? Whoever has seen me has seen the Father..." (John 14:9 ESV) There are many other verses that implicitly or explicitly proclaim that Jesus was God. In the same way, regarding the Holy Spirit, Jesus said in the book of John; "Nevertheless, I tell you the truth: it is to your advantage that I go away, for if I do not go away, the Helper *[Holy Spirit]* will not come to you. But if I go, I will send him to you." (John 16:7 ESV) In all this, we see the Son's relationship with the Father and Holy Spirit. But what is the Son's individual role?

The Gospels, especially the Gospel of John, have numerous verses that attribute all that Jesus is or does to "the one who sent me." Though Jesus has a unique role, it is important to note that this role is carried out under the authority and in complete and utter submission to the Father who sent Him.

> "I can do nothing on my own. As I hear, I judge, and my judgment is just, because I seek not my own will but the will of him who sent me." (John 5:30 ESV)

"For I have not spoken on my own authority, but the Father who sent me has himself given me a commandment—what to say and what to speak." (John 12:49 ESV)

So we know that Jesus is carrying out the will of His Father by the power of the Holy Spirit (Isaiah 11:2, 61:1-3; Luke 4:18-21). It is in this that we see the role of the second person of the Trinity. I think the Son's role could be summarized in four ways. Jesus is 1) the incarnation of God, who 2) led a life to lead, teach and communicate the redemptive will of God, 3) died to satisfy the wrath of God and pay the penalty for sin, and 4) was resurrected from the dead to overcome evil, provide newness of life, become our mediator with God, and rule and reign for all eternity. The work Jesus did provide the *justification, atonement, propitiation,* and *reconciliation* for our sin. We are *justified* (declared righteous); we received *atonement* and *reconciliation* (God allowed for our restoration and the satisfaction of our sin through the death of Christ on the cross); and we were *propitiated* (Christ gave us appeasement for our sins). These words are similar, but in combination, they emphasize the complete, encompassing, and thorough results achieved by the Son of God.

God The Holy Spirit

As we study the Trinity, it would be incorrect to state that the role of any one person within the Trinity is more important than the others. Without the three acting in complete harmony and fulfilling their individual roles, we would have no Christianity. The role of the Holy Spirit, however, should be of great significance to us as we see the Spirit's work in bringing us to faith, and we realize the Spirit's importance in the future as we aspire to grow in that same faith. In *Knowing God*, J.I. Packer said, "were it not for the work of the Holy Spirit there would be no gospel, no faith, no church, no Christianity in the world at all."[2]

The Holy Spirit is the most neglected and least understood person of the Trinity. In his sermon series, "The Essential Work of The Holy Spirit," John MacArthur, in reviewing the past and the present, shows that interest in the Holy Spirit has diminished significantly. He attributes this to the charismatic, pragmatic, and psychological movements in evangelical Christianity. In summary, MacArthur states:

> "Until here we are today, and it is a very rare thing to hear a message on the person of the Holy Spirit or the ministry of the Holy Spirit. On the one hand, we're reluctant to teach the truth, as over against the error that's so popular about the Holy Spirit. On the other hand, we aren't really

sure that the Holy Spirit is that critical to everything, because we're so good at what we do in terms of marketing and strategies, and we have figured out people so well with our psychological analysis that we know basically how to get to them and maybe the Holy Spirit's ministry isn't as critical as it once was."[3]

J. I. Packer, discussing the third person of the Trinity, put it this way:

> "…yet the person and work of the Holy Spirit are consistently ignored. The doctrine of the Holy Spirit is the Cinderella of Christian doctrines. Very few seem to be interested. But most (Christians), perhaps, do not think of the Holy Spirit at all, and have no positive ideas of any sort about what He does."[4]

We have briefly seen the Spirit's work in creation and the life and ministry of Christ, but what is His importance and influence on mankind in general and to God's elect in particular?

In an article, Dr. Charles Stanley provides a summary of the Trinity this way: "the Father creates a plan, Jesus Christ implements the plan, and the Holy Spirit administers the plan."[5] (*Administer* means to disperse and apply.) So, it is the role of the Holy Spirit to disperse and apply the plan of redemption and spiritual growth to believers. His role is to draw, convict, occupy, convert, regenerate, and sanctify God's elect. The Bible gives us the best depiction of these roles:

The Spirit Draws

> "No one can come to me unless the Father who sent me draws him. And I will raise him up on the last day." (John 6:44 ESV)

The Spirit Convicts

> "And when he comes, he will convict the world concerning sin and righteousness and judgment: concerning sin, because they do not believe in me; concerning righteousness, because I go to the Father, and you will see me no longer; concerning judgment, because the ruler of this world is judged." (John 16:8-11 ESV)

> "But when the Helper comes, whom I will send to you from the Father, the Spirit of truth, who proceeds from the Father, he will bear witness about me." (John 15:26 ESV)

The Spirit Occupies

> "Or do you not know that your body is a temple of the Holy Spirit within you, whom you have from God? You are not your own, for you were bought with a price. So glorify God in your body." (1 Corinthians 6:19-20 ESV)

The Spirit Converts and Regenerates

> "he saved us, not because of works done by us in righteousness, but according to his own mercy, by the washing of regeneration and renewal of the Holy Spirit," (Titus 3:5 ESV)

The Spirit Sanctifies

> "But we ought always to give thanks to God for you, brothers beloved by the Lord, because God chose you as the first-fruits to be saved, through sanctification by the Spirit and belief in the truth." (2 Thessalonians 2:13 ESV)

These verses show us that a Christian is brought to faith by the power of the Holy Spirit, who occupies us as believers in Christ. But our spiritual growth also relies upon the ministry of the Holy Spirit: "And those who belong to Christ Jesus have crucified the flesh with its passions and desires. If we live by the Spirit, let us also keep in step with the Spirit." (Galatians 5:24-25 ESV) If we belong to Christ, the Spirit now resides within us, and we have new spiritual life. But that's not all. We must also walk, or perhaps better stated, *learn* to walk, in the Spirit.

CHAPTER SEVEN

WALK IN THE SPIRIT

In the New Testament, Paul talks much about the battle that takes place between the flesh and spirit in the life of a believer. This battle is the process of our sanctification. How much of the old man have we discarded and how much of the new have we taken on? He tells us we need to discard, "sexual immorality, impurity, sensuality, idolatry, sorcery, enmity, strife, jealousy, fits of anger, rivalries, dissensions, divisions, envy, drunkenness, orgies, and things like these." and take on "the fruit of the Spirit… love, joy, peace, patience, kindness, goodness, faithfulness, gentleness, self-control…" (Galatians 5:19-23 ESV)

This is the battleground, and these are the forces that contend against one another. As we read this graphic, clear, and distinct description of the two opposing forces, we realize the importance of, and the emphasis placed on Paul's encouragement to walk in the Spirit and not the flesh.

> "But I say, walk by the Spirit, and you will not gratify the desires of the flesh. For the desires of the flesh are against the Spirit, and the desires of the Spirit are against the flesh, for these are opposed to each other, to keep you from doing the things you want to do." (Galatians 5:16-17 ESV)

As enlightened and as strong as Paul was in his relationship with God, he was no exception as a participant in the battle that rages in all of us as we attempt to emphasize the Spirit and produce His fruit. "So I find it to be a law that when I want to do right, evil lies close at hand. For I delight in the law of God, in my inner being, but I see in my members another law waging war against the law of my mind and making me captive to the law of sin that dwells in my members." (Romans 7:21-23 ESV)

As Paul instructs us, the critical aspect of all of this is to learn how to walk in the Spirit. What is it that allows us to produce the fruit of the Spirit and not the fruit of the flesh?

> "For if you live according to the flesh you will die, but if by the Spirit you put to death the deeds of the body, you will live. For all who are led by the Spirit of God are sons of God." (Romans 8:13-14 ESV)

The ability to walk in the Spirit is the result of our ongoing sanctification. We must learn and understand how we are to live this new life in Christ. This is done by the power of the Holy Spirit as we read, study, and pray over God's Word. God must continue to change our hearts so that we begin to act out what we know He would have us to do. We will be talking much more about this as we continue on in our study. Perhaps an example of what I am talking about might be of value.

One of the men I meet with weekly, in a discipling relationship, often discuss how we need to try and walk in the Spirit and produce the fruit of the Spirit daily. We are serious about this but often kid about making driving our cars an exception to the rule. Like many other things in life, it is hard to exhibit the fruit of the Spirit and give grace when someone cuts you off in heavy traffic. Knowing my wife, I told him that if that were to happen to her, she would probably feel like the driver had had a bad day and pray for them. When I got home and asked her that question in a serious way, that is exactly how she responded. Come on, give me a break! But in all seriousness, this is a great example of how we can either walk in the flesh or walk in the Spirit.

Our Position, Resources, and Power in Christ

There are some things we need to consider in our understanding, desire, and ability to walk in the Spirit. In his excellent sermon series on "Our Resources In

Christ"[1] and "The Fullness Of God"[2], John MacArthur focuses on some things that are essential to our success. We need to gain a clear understanding of our position, our resources, and our power in Christ.

As stated earlier, at one time we were alienated from God and dead in our trespasses and sins, but we were born again and made alive in Christ. As Colossians 2:13-15 (ESV) tells us, "And you, who were dead in your trespasses and the uncircumcision of your flesh, God made alive together with him, having forgiven us all our trespasses, by canceling the record of debt that stood against us with its legal demands. This he set aside, nailing it to the cross. He disarmed the rulers and authorities and put them to open shame, by triumphing over them in him."

What happened? We were changed and given a new position. "Therefore, if anyone is in Christ, he is a new creation. The old has passed away; behold, the new has come." (2 Corinthians 5:17 ESV) We are no longer our own, but we now belong to God. We are new. We reveled in this, we celebrated and were excited. But did we really, fully understand what had happened – what our new position was in relationship to God and the world around us? As life wore on, did we allow our flesh to overcome the revelation of this good news? To one degree or another, I would venture to say that the answers to these questions are *no* and *yes* respectively. Because of this, we need to take the time to gain a more thorough and complete understanding of our position, resources, and power in Christ.

So, what is this new position we have with God in Christ? What resources does it give us? What do we need to know and why is it important? Let's look at what the first chapter of Ephesians tells us:

> "Even as he chose us in him before the foundation of the world, that we should be holy and blameless before him. In love he predestined us for adoption to himself as sons through Jesus Christ, according to the purpose of his will, to the praise of his glorious grace, with which he has blessed us in the Beloved. In him we have redemption through his blood, the forgiveness of our trespasses, according to the riches of his grace, which he lavished upon us, in all wisdom and insight making known to us the mystery of his will, according to his purpose, which he set forth in Christ as a plan for the fullness of time, to unite all things in him, things in heaven and things on earth. In him we have obtained an inheritance, having been predestined according to the purpose of him who works all things according to the counsel of his will, so that we who were the first to hope in Christ might be to the praise of his glory. In him you also, when you heard the word of truth, the gospel of your

salvation, and believed in him, were sealed with the promised Holy Spirit, who is the guarantee of our inheritance until we acquire possession of it, to the praise of his glory." (Ephesians 1:4-14 ESV)

These verses help us to understand the resources and the incredible position of faith we have in Christ. Let's summarize what these verses tell us: 1) we were chosen and predestined; 2) we were adopted as sons; 3) we were blessed in the Beloved; 4) we were redeemed and forgiven; 5) we are heirs to the praise of His glory; and 6) we are sealed with the Holy Spirit. We could elaborate on each of these in detail, but the main point of them all is that we now belong to Christ who is the incarnation of the Almighty God, and that gives us a new position. It is not a trial period or test, temporary or fleeting, partial or incomplete. It does not depend on how we act, what we do or don't do, our gifts or talents, our strengths or weaknesses. This is our final, permanent, complete, unchanging, and eternal position that we have in Christ. These resources are always available.

If we could grasp this and more fully live this out in our lives, it would revolutionize our walk with the Lord and our impact on the world. It would be like being an heir to the throne of a monarch. We would walk, act and live out our position and its resources in a more obvious, meaningful, and intentional manner.

Why did Paul write these things to the Ephesian church? Because he wanted them to know their position in Christ and the power and resources that were made available to them, so they could learn to live and walk in this new faith that had been given to them. He prays to that end in the following verses:

> "I do not cease to give thanks for you, remembering you in my prayers, that the God of our Lord Jesus Christ, the Father of glory, may give you the Spirit of wisdom and of revelation in the knowledge of him, having the eyes of your hearts enlightened, that you may know what is the hope to which he has called you, what are the riches of his glorious inheritance in the saints, and what is the immeasurable greatness of his power toward us who believe, according to the working of his great might." (Ephesians 1:16-19 ESV)

Paul wants them to know and understand who they are in Christ. He wants them to know this so they can live it out – to know "the hope to which He has called you." To know "the riches of His glorious inheritance." To know "the immeasurable greatness of his power toward us who believe."

Paul prays for the "wisdom and revelation in the knowledge of Him" so that we would begin to understand the position and resources we have in Christ.

These are the resources that are made available to us as believers – the things we possess as a result of our election. *Resources* are something we use to get a job done. In this sense, Christ is our resource. We have everything we need in Him. He is the source of all wisdom, knowledge, and revelation, by His Word and the power of the Holy Spirit. We must know these things so that we can walk in them and live them out in our lives.

Why is this important to study and know? Because this understanding will help us realize the victory we have already attained against the flesh. It will help us live out this victory and produce the fruit of the Spirit in our lives. There is much more but comprehending this is essential to our ability to walk in the Spirit.

CHAPTER EIGHT
KEYS TO WALKING IN THE SPIRIT

We have talked about the significance of learning to grow in God and walk in the Spirit, but there are a few other aspects of this that we need to consider as well. Since they are critical to our success, we will call them the *keys* to walking in the Spirit.

Walking in Grace

Grace is another word that we tend to use in a common or casual manner. We know we are saved by it, but what meaning does it have in our lives after that? I love the Acronym for G.R.A.C.E.: **G**od's **R**iches **A**t **C**hrist's **E**xpense. But even in this, it can tend to become more of a colloquial expression and lose its more serious and significant meaning. What is *grace*? What does it really mean, and how does it work?

    The word can be defined in different ways, but for our purposes, we might generally define it as *the supernatural power of God imposed upon mankind.* It is something that God provides to allow and sustain life on the earth. We have *common grace* that is extended to all creation, and we have *efficacious grace* that is applied to God's elect. By God's plan, we are not all saved, but all receive mercy until we are judged. This may not seem fair, but that is a topic for another study.

Ephesians tells us, "for by grace you have been saved through faith. And this is not your own doing; it is the gift of God, not a result of works, so that no one may boast." (Ephesians 2:8-9 ESV) The *grace* used in this passage is *efficacious grace*. It's called that because it is *effective immediately* in bringing someone to saving faith. Though inscrutable to us, it is an act of God solely dependent *on* God by His sovereign will.

Not only are we saved by grace, but we also must learn to walk in this grace as we lead a Christian life. This is where grace tends to become more obscure. Just as we realized that it was grace that saved us, we must also understand that it is by this same grace that we need to lead the Christian life. It's critical to our sanctification.

It is by **G**ods **R**iches **A**t **C**hrist's **E**xpense that we live and move and have our being in this life. We must recognize our continuing and total dependence on Christ. We must remember that it is the bloodied, mutilated, and now resurrected body of Christ on that Roman cross that brought us into relationship with God. It is that same body that sustains us and allows us to overcome the evil, difficulties, and challenges of this world. We must learn to apply this to our lives if we are to produce the fruit of the Spirit and experience victory in Christ.

When we walk in grace, we remember Christ's atoning act of forgiveness for our sins on the cross and the promise of eternal life. If we try to walk in the realization of what has been done for us, we should more quickly extend this same grace to others. Perhaps the example of getting cut off in heavy traffic works to demonstrate this as well (though I wish it didn't)!

Learning The Lesson of God's Sovereignty

Until recently, I had never thought about God's sovereignty as a lesson to be learned. This came about while reading Jerry Bridges' book, *The Fruitful Life*, in the chapter on Joy. Bridges used the Old Testament book of Job as an example of how we deal with difficulties in life that test our faith. Bridges stated:

> "At the beginning of [Job's] testing, he reacted positively with the statement, "The Lord gives and the Lord has taken away; May the name of the Lord be praised" (Job 1:21). But as time wore on and the trials, aggravated by the false accusations of his friends continued, Job's faith and patience gave out. He was finally reduced to saying, "It profits a man nothing when he tries to please God" (Job 34:9). But though Job's faith

wore out, God's faithfulness did not. He stayed with Job until Job had learned *the lesson of God's sovereignty…*"[1].

At the end of the book, Job replies to God, "I know that you can do all things, and that no purpose of yours can be thwarted. 'Who is this that hides counsel without knowledge?' Therefore I have uttered what I did not understand, things too wonderful for me, which I did not know." (Job 42:2-3 ESV)

Like Job, we must also learn the lesson of God's sovereignty, so that when we are hard pressed, surrounded by the difficulties and trials of life, we can move forward, come to the same conclusion, and affirm what Romans 8:28 (ESV) tells us: "And we know that for those who love God all things work together for good, for those who are called according to his purpose." Job had lost everything, but in the end, he received back what he had lost twofold. God was very gracious to Job, but this cannot be our motivation or expectation. God may not choose to restore us in this way. What was it that motivated and encouraged the apostle Paul, making him sing and praise God while in prison, display true joy amid beatings, hardships, stoning, rejection, and serve others while shipwrecked? It was his spiritual maturity in Christ and his love and trust in a God who he knew was sovereign over all things.

I think this lesson is an essential part of growing in God and learning to walk in the Spirit. Otherwise, our reaction to life in this sin-filled world will only lead to anger, frustration, anxiety, depression, and perhaps much worse. The only fruit we will bear is that which comes from our flesh.

In addition, it can be easy for us to *say* that we are going to trust in and rely on God, but are we truly turning our lives over to His sovereign will? Are we ready to experience whatever that means? Paul was! He said; "For to me, to live is Christ, and to die is gain," (Philippians 1:21 ESV)

Are we ready to live out our faith like that? If we are honest, I don't think we really are. Not only that, but I think what we really want God to do is work out His plan according to our selfish wants and desires. When this isn't happening, we can easily become frustrated, anxious, bitter, angry, and upset. For any of us, this could be our initial reaction, but for a mature Christian, it should be short lived. At some point, we should acknowledge God's sovereignty and move into a position of F.A.I.T.H. (**F**orsaking **A**ll, **I** **T**rust **H**im).

One of the more deceptive ways we refuse to rely on God is when we get angry, down on ourselves, moody, or depressed, and we somehow think this is okay. *I have a right to respond in this way. God will understand.* And believe me, God does. But what we don't often realize is that this is an egregious sin against a holy God. What we have done in behaving this way is to show our unbelief. We are not living in the victory that Christ has given us on the cross when we do this; instead, we are showing defeat and submission to the enemy. We are making it all about us and not about God at all. We are going against, at the very least, the first three commandments: "You shall have no other gods before me," "You shall not make for yourself a carved image," and "You shall not take the name of the Lord your God in vain..." (Deuteronomy 5:7-11 ESV) When we do this, we become *practical atheists*, believing in God but acting like we don't. So again, our maturity in Christ and our understanding of God's sovereignty is critical.

When we show unbelief, we are not trusting in God and His Word. But often, we do this without realizing it. If we have a true situation of unbelief, then we need to go back and study God's Word. We need to pray and seek godly counsel.

Total Responsibility, Total Dependance

It is important to understand the process God uses to grow us spiritually. As we have seen, salvation is a supernatural, independent, efficacious act of God. But our sanctification is a different matter. Ongoing spiritual growth relies on what is called a *synergistic relationship* with God. This means that it takes both God and us to grow. We must cooperate *together* in the process.

The basic idea about a synergistic relationship is that the combined results of two or more individuals, working together, exceeds what they could have produced individually. The quantity and quality of the result is key, and it determines if working together or separately is the best option.

This is not the case in our situation. The result (our sanctification) is critically reliant upon a synergistic relationship with the Holy Spirit. If we try to work outside of this, we will not succeed. In our relationship with God, we are both *totally responsible* and *totally dependent*. What does this mean?

In *The Fruitful Life*, Jerry Bridges put it this way: "Though the power for Christlike character comes from Christ, the responsibility for developing and displaying that character is ours… We need to learn that the Bible teaches both total responsibility and total dependence."[2] The common error we make is to favor one over the other. We tend to put all the responsibility on either ourselves or on God. Having grown up in a very self-centered, independent world, we have been conditioned to believe that all we must do is work harder, smarter, or longer. Either that, or we believe we can rely entirely on God's grace – that He will do it all for us. In either case, we ignore scripture and open ourselves up to sin. Bridges stated it this way: "One day we sense our personal responsibility and seek to live a godly life by the strength of our own willpower. The next day, realizing the futility of trusting ourselves, we turn it all over to Christ and abdicate our responsibility, which is set forth in the scriptures."[3] We become either overly self-reliant or slothful. The proper balance we want to attain is found in Philippians 2:12-13 (ESV):

> "Therefore, my beloved, as you have always obeyed, so now, not only as in my presence but much more in my absence, work out your own salvation with fear and trembling, for it is God who works in you, both to will and to work for his good pleasure."

Using commentary from several sources, Bridges goes on to state that these verses are telling us that we are called to persistently pursue our own spiritual life – which is only done by the active participation of God. To put it more succinctly, "it is our duty to grow in Grace." Responsibility and dependence are two sides of the same coin.

How do we keep the proper balance between responsibility and dependence? We strive to learn, grow and pursue our sanctification in Christ. It is only with constant diligence and discipline that we have any chance. We will waver and even fail at times, but we must get back up, dust ourselves off and begin again. Remember that even this is done only by the sovereign grace of God.

CHAPTER NINE

MOTIVATION AND COMMITMENT

Motivation

We should always consider our motivation in anything we undertake in our lives. We probably don't think of it as a fundamental aspect of any plan or activity. In many cases, it is probably just something we take for granted.

Motivation is often expressed as the energy, passion, or purpose behind why we do something – the impetus which creates the desire to keep going and finish whatever it is that we've started. It may even be our whole reason for being, pushing us forward and keeping us from becoming discouraged, the ingredient that provides the drive and purpose for our endeavors. A lack of motivation may result from physical or mental tiredness, or more serious concerns like depression, fear, anxiety, and loss of purpose and hope.

Before we discuss it further, let's first try and define what it is. Probably one of the more simpler definitions I found was, "the reason or reasons one has for acting or behaving in a particular way."[1]

Positivepsychology.com describes motivation in the following way:

> "Motivation is an internal process. Whether we define it as a drive or a need, motivation is a condition inside us that desires a change...when we tap into this well of energy, motivation endows the person with the drive, and direction needed to engage... with an adaptive, open-ended, and problem-solving sort of way... The essence of motivation is energized and persistent goal-directed behavior. When we are motivated we move and take action. Motivation is influenced by satisfaction of needs that are either necessary for sustaining life or essential for wellbeing or growth."[2]

If we desire to grow in God and His Word, we must consider our motives for doing so. We need to examine ourselves and try to determine and ensure we have the *right* motives. The underlying idea is to ask ourselves why we are doing something, and to keep asking that *why?* until we get to the root reason. If that reason does not point to God, then we need to go back, reassess our purpose, and start over.

In *The Fruitful Life*, Jerry Bridges states that "devotion to God is the only acceptable motive for actions that are pleasing to God."[3] This, of course, applies to everything we do, and growing in God is no exception. As Bridges points out, "too often our motives are self-centered rather than God-centered."[4] We want to feel good about ourselves or gain more knowledge to impress others. He points out the good examples of Joseph and Potiphar's wife, and Abraham and Isaac. As well, when Jesus taught about the law and the prophets hanging on the commandments to love God and love your neighbor, "he was teaching not merely that those two commandments of love sum up all the other commandments but rather that all the other commandments depend on the motivation of love for their fulfillment[5]... All of our actions, to be acceptable to God, must be done out of a sense of devotion to God."[6] Without the proper motivation, our efforts are of no value, no matter how honorable or righteous they may seem. If we are to grow in God, we must have the right motivation: the desire to love, honor, glorify, and worship the Lord.

Our Commitment

The next thing we need to consider is commitment. What does real commitment look like, and how should it relate to our motivation to grow in God? Too often we use the word *commitment* in a casual and insincere manner. We may have good intentions, but we often fall short of whatever it was we said we would do. *Commitment* is a word that implies formal agreement and is built on trust, but we are prone to break our pledges and renege on what we agreed we would do. What are some inherent problems found in this type of commitment? We have not considered our schedule, our resources, or our abilities, and we have not made a plan. On the other side of the fence, the thing we have committed to is often vague, unclear, poorly communicated, or left to our own interpretation.

Before we talk about commitment in relation to growing in God, let's more formally define what it means. The dictionary tells us that commitment is "the state or quality of being dedicated to a cause or activity."[7] Similar words are *devotion, allegiance, loyalty* and *faithfulness*. This list gives us a better idea of the importance and significance of this word. More importantly, the thought of who we are making our commitment to, should sober us and bring serious contemplation about what we are getting ready to commit to.

In his book *The Discipline of Grace*, Jerry Bridges talks about growing in God as "the pursuit of holiness." In the first chapter, "How Good Is Good Enough," he states, "The Holy Spirit's work in transforming us more and more into the likeness of Christ is called sanctification. Our involvement and cooperation with Him in His work is what I call the pursuit of holiness...The pursuit of holiness requires sustained and vigorous effort. It allows for no indolence, no lethargy, no halfhearted commitment, and no laissez faire attitude toward even the smallest sins. In short, it demands the highest priority in the life of a Christian, because to be holy is to be like Christ, God's goal for every Christian."[8]

I think we can see the importance and seriousness of using this word in our pledge to obey God's command to grow in our relationship with Him. Yet how do we practically state what our commitment is and what it will look like? If we have satisfied the *why*, then what we need to continue to do is establish the practical aspects of *how*, *when* and *where*.

CHAPTER TEN

DISCIPLESHIP

"Go therefore and make disciples of all
nations, baptizing them in the name of the Father
and of the Son and of the Holy Spirit,"
(Matthew 28:19 ESV)

The *how* of growing in God is multifaceted, so before we get too detailed, it might be a good time to talk about *discipleship*. This word is frequently used when we talk about evangelism and growing in God, but do we really have a clear understanding of its meaning or an idea of how to carry it out? I have always been somewhat unclear about what discipleship really was and feel some clarification is needed.

Discipleship is composed of two words: "disciple" and "ship". There are many other words that do this as well, like *friendship, internship, dictatorship,* and *apprenticeship*. I found that when "ship" is used in this way, it is considered a *noun suffix*, which changes the meaning of a noun into a new noun in one of the following ways: first, the state or condition of being (or becoming), as in *friendship*; second, the position, status, or duties of something or someone, as in *internship*; and lastly, the skill or ability of someone or something, as in *horsemanship*.[1] I think *discipleship* falls primarily into the first category: the state or condition of being or becoming, in our case, a disciple.

Simply speaking, discipleship is the ongoing activity, or process involved, in becoming and remaining a disciple. The important word that needs definition is the word *disciple*. Once this is done, you can then define the process necessary to make one.

The Bible states this in Matthew 28:19 (ESV) when Jesus says, "Go therefore and make disciples of all nations, baptizing them in the name of the Father and of the Son and of the Holy Spirit." The phrase *make disciples* is, in essence, discipleship, but must also include the necessary elements of doing this as we go (*go therefore*) and of multiplying (*all nations*).

A disciple is a follower of Christ – one who aspires to follow the teachings, lifestyle, and behavior of Christ. As Paul states, "be imitators of me, as I am of Christ." (1 Corinthians 11:1 ESV) If you are a follower of Christ, you are a *disciple* and should be involved in ongoing *discipleship*. Our spiritual growth and sanctification are inherent within this process. So what then are we to be doing?

There are a lot of different ideas and opinions about what is included in discipleship and how discipleship should be conducted. I thought Jerry Bridges' book, *The Discipline of Grace*, did a good job of breaking it down into its various components. He states:

> "As believers we are continually challenged with the demands and duties of discipleship. These demands and duties include such things as 1. the spiritual disciplines (quiet time, Bible study, prayer, worship, church attendance, and so on); 2. obedience to God's moral will set forth in the Bible or, as I call it, the pursuit of holiness; and 3. service or ministry for the Kingdom of God. Almost everything we need to do as believers is probably included in the three words disciplines, holiness, and service."[2] (numbers added)

As I studied this material, I was once again challenged to think about what I was trying to accomplish through this writing. Reading this section of Jerry's book helped me realize that my focus is on *holiness,* or perhaps better stated, *personal holiness* – personal sanctification and growth – hence the title, *Growing in God.* This is not to preclude or reduce the importance of the other aspects of discipleship Bridges discusses, but I believe an emphasis on personal holiness is a pre-cursor to effective execution of the "spiritual disciplines" as well as "service or ministry."

This does not mean that holiness cannot develop and grow out of the spiritual disciplines or service, but it seems that development and growth in personal holiness would be a more natural beginning and priority. If we are not rooted and grounded in our personal relationship with God, which provides the necessary motivation and commitment, the results of the other aspects of discipleship may become more physically dutiful, religious, or legalistic in nature.

Obviously, all areas of discipleship will occur concurrently. But if we prioritize, emphasize, and teach about our personal responsibility to grow in holiness, we may avoid these pitfalls I just mentioned. I think it would be fair to say that the development of this type of growth is severely neglected today in the life of the believer. So, at this point, we need to take time to discuss what Bridges calls "The Pursuit of Holiness." Before we do that, though, let's talk about some questions we might have when it comes to the word *discipleship*. I believe we covered questions dealing with the overall definition of discipleship and what it looks like, so let's go on to some others:

Is there a difference between discipleship and sanctification?

I think the difference here is that discipleship is the process we follow, and sanctification is the result we are seeking to achieve. As believers, we should be eager to learn and grow in our faith (*discipleship*) so that we can know God more and obey His command to become holy and set apart for His special use and purpose (our *sanctification*). As Jesus was set apart and sent (*sanctified*) for God's special purpose, we are commanded to do likewise.

> Gotquestions.org comments:
>
> ""Progressive" or "experiential" sanctification, as it is sometimes called, is the effect of obedience to the Word of God in ones life. It is the same as growing in the Lord or spiritual maturity (2 Peter 3:18 ESV). God started the work of making us like Christ (positional sanctification), and He is continuing it (Philippians 1:6 ESV). This type of sanctification is to be pursued by the believer earnestly (1 Peter 1:15; Hebrews 12:14) and is effected (sic) by the application of the Word (John 17:17). Progressive sanctification has in view the setting apart of believers for the purpose for which they are sent into the world: "As you sent me into the world, I have sent them into the world. For them I sanctify myself, that they too may be truly sanctified" (John 17:18-19). That Jesus set Himself apart for God's purpose is both the basis and the condition of our being set apart (see John 10:36). We are sanctified and sent because Jesus was. Our Lords sanctification is the pattern of and power for our own. The sending and the sanctifying are

inseparable. On this account we are called "saints" (hagioi in the Greek) or "sanctified ones." Prior to salvation, our behavior bore witness to our standing in the world in separation from God, but now our behavior should bear witness to our standing before God in separation from the world. Little by little, every day, "those who are being sanctified" (Hebrews 10:14, ESV) are becoming more like Christ."[3]

Can I disciple myself?

I believe the objective answer to this question is no. Though much personal time and study are necessary and required for successful discipleship, it must be done in relationship with others in the body of Christ. (See section on Relationships, Commitment, and Accountability)

Is evangelism part of discipleship?

Going and making disciples is what the great commission is all about (see Matthew 28:19-20) and is a mandate to all believers. This includes evangelism, because we must first present the Gospel unto salvation and then disciple those who confess belief, knowing that only God can bring them to true saving faith. In that sense, discipleship should always include ongoing evangelism. I think, however, that evangelism is perhaps more aimed at gospel presentation and initial conversion of the prospective believer, whereas discipleship is more concerned with the development, maturity, and sanctification of the converted believer.

How do I make a disciple?

God, ultimately, is the disciple-maker, but He uses us to evangelize and sanctify others. There have been many books and opinions expressed on how to do this, but I think the short answer is spending time with others to assist them in growing in their relationship with God – much of what this book is all about!

When I become a Christian, am I considered a disciple?

Well, technically, yes. But perhaps the better question would be, *am I an active disciple? Am I pursuing an on-going, intentional and committed plan to grow in my relationship with God?* If the answer is *no*, and if it has been this way for some time, you are either in violation of God's mandate to grow or you may not even be a true believer. This has been previously discussed in the section "Am I Really Saved" in chapter three.

CHAPTER ELEVEN

HOLINESS

I think the idea of holiness scares and intimidates most of us. We view holiness as sacrosanct, something far beyond us in terms of value and importance. It is not something we feel we could ever be associated with or attain. It is reserved exclusively for God and God alone. In a sermon on holiness, R.C. Sproul quoted Rudolph Otto, who in his book, *The Idea of The Holy*, called holiness the "*Mysterium Tremendum*" – the tremendous mystery. That pretty much sums it up. But at the same time, the Bible commands us to be holy. It is for this reason that we need to explore holiness more deeply and try and discover its true meaning for the believer.

Let's first talk about God's holiness. It is impossible for us to have adequate words to define the holiness of God, so we need to seek help from the Bible.

Isaiah tells us that in the year King Uzziah died, the Prophet had a vision of the Lord seated on a throne with the seraphim flying above Him and calling to one another, "Holy, holy, holy is the Lord Almighty; the whole earth is full of his glory!" (Isaiah 6:3 NIV)

The word of extreme emphasis in this passage is the word *holy* – in Hebrew, *kadosh*. We know this because the word is used three times in a row. It's like a musical crescendo with the loudness of a triple forte: *Holy, Holy, Holy*. *Kadosh* means "*other*" or "*set apart*". This defines an exclusive and unique quality to the subject of the phrase – in this case, "the Lord Almighty." He is set apart, but He is also defined as *Lord* and *Almighty*. To the adjectives of exclusivity and uniqueness, we must also add *sovereign Lord* and *King*. So God, in this sense, is an exceptional being. All in all, we will never find the words to adequately define or describe Him. This is difficult because we do not live in the same realm, the same space, or the same time that He does. He is unique and without equal. He is the definer of life, the creator of all existence. R.C. Sproul states "that which is holy is "other" or different from something else – it refers to God's transcendence or magnificence – higher and superior to all other things. That which is holy is different, set a part from all other things."[2]

> "He stretches out the north over the void and hangs the earth on nothing. He binds up the waters in his thick clouds, and the cloud is not split open under them. He covers the face of the full moon and spreads over it his cloud. He has

inscribed a circle on the face of the waters at the boundary between light and darkness. The pillars of heaven tremble and are astounded at his rebuke. By his power he stilled the sea; by his understanding he shattered Rahab. By his wind the heavens were made fair; his hand pierced the fleeing serpent. Behold, these are but the outskirts of his ways, and how small a whisper do we hear of him! But the thunder of his power who can understand?" (Job 26:7-14 ESV)

"Who is like you, O Lord, among the gods? Who is like you, majestic in holiness, awesome in glorious deeds, doing wonders?" (Exodus 15:11 ESV)

With much more that could be said, this is the Holiness of God. So what is the level of holiness that we are to attain? What does scripture mean when it says, "be holy as I am holy"?

Personal Holiness

In his sermon, Sproul goes on to state that "what makes something holy is the touch of God upon it. When the one who Himself is other and different touches that which is ordinary it becomes extraordinary. When He touches us we become uncommon."[3] But I don't think we are uncommon in the same sense that God is.

As we have already seen, when God saves us, we are imputed with His righteousness. He sees us not as we are, but through the righteousness of His Son. In this positional sense, we could also be considered holy; but it is the ongoing holiness – perhaps we should call it *practical holiness* – that we are at this point most concerned with. In the same sense that we are called to walk in the Spirit, put on the new man of Christ, and pursue sanctification, we are also called to "be holy." When we are called to *be holy*, we are called to be *different*, like He is different, by His example. We need to understand, grow into, and continue to pursue what this difference represents throughout our lives.

The Bible, once again, is our source of wisdom and understanding. The New Testament instructs us and helps us understand the idea and purpose of holiness in our lives.

Our Encouragement and Incentive

> "But now that you have been set free from sin and have become slaves of God, the fruit you get leads to sanctification and its end, eternal life." (Romans 6:22 ESV)

> "For they disciplined us for a short time as it seemed best to them, but he disciplines us for our good, that we may share his holiness." (Hebrews 12:10 ESV)

"Since we have these promises, beloved, let us cleanse ourselves from every defilement of body and spirit, bringing holiness to completion in the fear of God." (2 Corinthians 7:1 ESV)

"Assuming that you have heard about him and were taught in him, as the truth is in Jesus, to put off your old self, which belongs to your former manner of life and is corrupt through deceitful desires, and to be renewed in the spirit of your minds, and to put on the new self, created after the likeness of God in true righteousness and holiness." (Ephesians 4:21-24 ESV)

The Necessity or Requirement of Holiness

"Strive for peace with everyone, and for the holiness without which no one will see the Lord." (Hebrews 12:14 ESV)

Setting Ourselves Apart unto the Lord

"For I am the Lord your God. Consecrate yourselves therefore, and be holy, for I am holy." (Leviticus 11:44a ESV)

"I appeal to you therefore, brothers, by the mercies of God, to present your bodies as a living sacrifice, holy and acceptable to God, which is your spiritual worship. Do not be conformed to this world, but be transformed by the renewal of your mind, that by testing you may discern what is the will of God, what is good and acceptable and perfect." (Romans 12:1-2 ESV)

The Purpose of Our Election

"Even as he chose us in him before the foundation of the world, that we should be holy and blameless before him..." (Ephesians 1:4 ESV)

"For God has not called us for impurity, but in holiness." (1 Thessalonians 4:7 ESV)

"You shall be holy to me, for I the Lord am holy and have separated you from the peoples, that you should be mine." (Leviticus 20:26 ESV)

Moral Behavior

"Consecrate yourselves, therefore, and be holy, for I am the Lord your God. Keep my statutes and do them; I am the Lord who sanctifies you." (Leviticus 20:7-8 ESV)

It is clear from these verses that we have a strong mandate, encouragement, and incentive to pursue holiness. But what more specifically and concretely is this holiness that we are talking about?

In his book, *The Pursuit of Holiness*, Jerry Bridges helps answer this question. He states:

> "The idea of exactly how to be holy has suffered from many false concepts. In some circles, holiness is equated with a series of specific prohibitions... When we follow this approach to holiness we are in danger of becoming like the Pharisees with their endless lists of trivial do's and don'ts, and their self-righteous attitude... for others, it means unattainable perfection, an idea that fosters either delusion or discouragement about one's sin.
> All of these ideas, while accurate to some degree, miss the true concept. To be holy is to be morally blameless. It is to be separated from sin and, therefore, consecrated to God. The word signifies "separation to God, and the conduct befitting those so separated.
> Perhaps the best way of understanding the concept of holiness is to note how writers of the New Testament used the word. In 1 Thessalonians 4:3-7, Paul used the term in contrast to a life of immorality and impurity.

> Peter used it in contrast to living according to the evil desires we had when we lived outside of Christ (1 Peter 1:14-16). John contrasted one who is holy with those who do wrong and are vile (Revelation 22:1). To live a holy life, then, is to live a life in conformity to the moral precepts of the Bible and in contrast to the sinful ways of the world. It is to live a life characterized by the "[putting] off of your old self, which is being corrupted by its deceitful desires…and [putting] on the new self, created to be like God in true righteousness and holiness" (Ephesians 4:22, 24)".[4]

The pursuit of holiness is, in short, the ongoing learning and obedience to the moral commandments, statues, and rules of the Bible. It is not some mystical concept only revealed to certain highly devout Christians. It is reading, studying, meditating, and praying through God's Word, receiving the truth and revelation of scripture by the power of the Holy Spirit. We then apply this to our lives through our reason and intellect, in our daily walk and life in the world, seeking to honor God and be a witness to the truth. The *how* of this is the often-deferred process that is essential to our success: addressing our sin.

CHAPTER TWELVE

SIN

There are many people who don't think they sin. They believe this way because they feel they are basically "good" and that any indiscretion they have committed should be overlooked and not counted against them. They set their own standard for right and wrong. They don't consider God's standard or His point of view. As we have already seen, this only creates relative morality and a justification for doing whatever a person feels is right in their own eyes.

They also feel that if God is going to hold these kinds of things against them, then this is not a "god" they want to be a part of or serve. They believe this way because, in many cases, they don't understand sin from a biblical perspective. They do not understand that the sin of Adam and Eve, committed in the garden, was passed down to all of us (Romans 5:12) and resulted in *separation* (spiritual death) between God and mankind. Fortunately, God provided a remedy for this by sending His one and only son to die on a cross to pay the penalty for our sins. Once we see our sin in this way and accept Jesus as the payment for our sins, are we truly forgiven and brought back into a right and living spiritual relationship with God. As we have already discussed, comprehending the holiness of God is key to this understanding as well.

In a broad sense, the word *sin* can be used to denote any act that goes against defined laws, rules, codes of conduct, or moral behaviors. From a spiritual or biblical perspective, sin is anything that goes against God and His authority. When Adam and Eve sinned in the garden, the sin itself was wrong, but more importantly, they disobeyed the authority of God. One dictionary I found, defined sin as, "an immoral act considered to be a transgression against divine law."[1] So sin is not so much about going against the law of man but the law of a divine, transcendent God. We should be most concerned with what we have done against God.

Writing a section on sin, for the edification of the Christian believer, was somewhat of a second thought for me. I felt that sin was a topic that most of us were familiar with. All I needed to do was come up with a simple definition, provide some discussion, Bible verses, and examples on the topic, and move forward. But when I attempted to do this, I struggled. I was not able to find the words and felt like I could not express what I was trying to say completely and thoroughly. I wanted it simple, straightforward, and quick. I had other more important things to write about. But, as God has done before in this writing, He would not let me be content or satisfied in a cursory discussion of sin.

As I tried, yet another time, to complete this section, I randomly opened Jerry Bridges' book, *The Disciplines of Grace*, and looked down at a chapter subtitle which read "The Seriousness of Sin."[2] As I began to read, I realized why I was having so much difficulty writing this section. As you may have already guessed, I wasn't taking sin seriously enough. God was saying to my heart, *you need to study this more. You need to understand more deeply what this simple three letter word means*. As I continued to read, I quickly wrote this note to myself: *why is sin so important to growing in God?* I guess I had a preconceived idea that we grow by studying the positive aspects of our faith. We deal generally with sin but more specifically and importantly with our redemption, becoming more like Christ, and taking on and displaying the fruit of the Spirit (love, joy, peace, patience, kindness, goodness, faithfulness, gentleness, and self-control). But as important as these things may be, we must also understand the underlying reasons why these things aren't already a part of our character.

If we wrote about the most rebellious, evil, perverted, deadly, dangerous, threatening, contagious, destructive, tortuous, menacing, immoral, hateful force in the universe, it might get our personal, undivided attention. For this is what sin is, and probably much, much more. Sin is not so much about what we do but who we are doing it to, or perhaps more accurately, "against." We are rebelling against God's authority, His sovereign right to rule and reign as creator, King, and Lord of all things. In *The Disciplines of Grace*, Bridges uses three words to emphasize the gravity of sin in this regard: *rebellion*, *despise*, and *defy*.[3]

Rebellion

When we go against God and His Word, we are rebelling against His authority. We are telling God that we have a better plan, that His Word is of no value to us, and that we are going to do it our way. We are committing idolatry – self-worship. We are placing our own ideas and beliefs above God, placing ourselves in a preeminent position to God. We are blaspheming His Holy name by showing contempt and irreverence for Him. Rebellion began with Adam and Eve. They were not content to do it God's way. They went against His authority. As a result, the whole human race has been tainted with their sin and separated spiritually from God.

Despise

Despise is an extremely strong word. We may say that we don't like something or that we even hate something, but to *despise* is to take the idea of disfavor to the ultimate extreme. Dictionary.com gives the definition of despise as: "to regard with contempt, distaste, disgust, or disdain; scorn; loathe."[4] This is what we do to God and His word when we sin. In *Disciplines of Grace*, using David's sin with Bathsheba as an example of how David's sin was despising God, Bridges says:

> "We cannot evade the force of the word despise, thinking it fits the scandalous nature of David's crimes but doesn't apply to us. The same God who said, "You shall not murder" or "You shall not commit adultery" also said "You shall not covet" (Exodus 20:13-14,17). It is not the seriousness of the sin as we view it, but the infinite majesty and sovereignty of the God who gave the commands, that make our sin a despising of God and His Word."[5]

Defy

To *defy* something or someone is to initiate open resistance and refuse any level of obedience or cooperation. I think the word goes beyond a particular noun, implying complete rejection of a philosophy, purpose, or reasoning. It is a desire not only to negate something, but to replace it with an opposite attitude and opinion. It's associated with disobedience, but defiance goes much further. It confronts, spurns, and violates. Bridges describes this word from its use in 1 Kings 13:21 – "You have defied the Word of the Lord"[6]. He states that the word *disobeyed* is often used as a substitute for *defy* in other Bible translations, but it does not capture the intense force of this word, probably because we are so used to the concept of disobedience. "But we all recognize that the word defy escalates the seriousness of disobedience. It is a direct challenge to authority."[7] I think of the contrast between a child who would just not do what you asked in disobedience, compared to the attitude of a child who displays outward defiance. In a like manner, as children of God, our sin defies God's authority over us.

To have an adequate understanding of sin, however, we must trace its progression, biblically, in the life of the believer – from its inception to its positional demise to its ongoing reduction and ultimate elimination. This is essential to our pursuit of personal holiness and to grow in our relationship with God. The book of Romans helps us understand this better.

As we have already seen from Romans 5:12, no one escapes the indictment of sin. The word *indictment* has a surprisingly appropriate secular definition: "a formal charge or accusation of a serious crime; a thing that serves to illustrate that a system or situation is bad and deserves condemnation."[8] This is what happened to us as a result of Adam's sin – we were indicted. We deserve God's condemnation. As Romans 3:23 tells us, "all have sinned and fall short of God's glory." So, whether we agree with this idea or want to argue with it, it remains a biblical fact that we cannot escape. But there is good news for this unfortunate reality. As Romans 8:1

(ESV) goes on to tell us, "there is therefore now no condemnation for those who are in Christ Jesus." God provided a way out of our predicament.

As a result of our belief and salvation in Christ, we escape the condemnation of God. He now sees us through the righteousness of His Son and imputes this to our account. It would be great if this was all there was to it, but Romans 6 helps us better understand the exact position in which we now stand:

> "What shall we say then? Are we to continue in sin that grace may abound? By no means! How can we who died to sin still live in it? Do you not know that all of us who have been baptized into Christ Jesus were baptized into his death? We were buried therefore with him by baptism into death, in order that, just as Christ was raised from the dead by the glory of the Father, we too might walk in newness of life...So you also must consider yourselves dead to sin and alive to God in Christ Jesus. Let not sin therefore reign in your mortal body, to make you obey its passions. Do not present your members to sin as instruments for unrighteousness, but present yourselves to God as those who have been brought from death to life, and your members to God as instruments for righteousness." (Romans 6:1-4, 11-13 ESV)

As we see in these verses, it is incumbent upon us to begin to walk in this new man of righteousness. Though the old man is dead, he still clings to us like a corpse attached to the outside of our bodies. We have been given a new life, but the passion of our sin nature still draws us back to our old sinful ways. We were not only baptized into a new life in Christ; we were also baptized into His death.

As Christ was raised from death to life, we must also be raised to newness of life and learn to walk in it. The "old man" was crucified with Him so that the body of sin might be done away with – killed, mortified – so that we would not continue to be a slave to sin.

Though not necessarily intended for this purpose, Romans 7 offers an illustration that we can use to help our understanding of these verses. It tells the story of a woman who would be considered an adulterer if she marries another man while her current husband is still alive; however, she would be free to marry again if he had already died.

If she remarries but continues to live in the past, thinking and acting out her life as if she is still married to a dead man, she is fooling herself and is not in active pursuit of a new life with a new husband. To have a successful new life, she must somehow "put off" and put away the old relationship. She must not actively pursue the old life while living in a new life.

This is what can happen to us as believers in Christ. We are dead to the old man of sin and have been made alive as the new man of righteousness, but we tend to live in the old man. He wants to cling to, reign over, and rule us. We must not allow this to happen. We must actively and intentionally identify the sins of the old man and kill them. Like the newly married woman, we must immerse ourselves in our new relationship with Christ, constantly putting it on, so there is no room in our lives for the old dead man of sin. This is necessary for our sanctification and allows us to grow and actively pursue holiness.

After all of this, I hope that we have a better concept and appreciation for sin and its seriousness. But the big question, as I asked earlier, is this: what does sin have to do with growing in God and the pursuit of holiness? As God has helped me realize: everything.

We've talked about several reasons why we need to grow in God and pursue holiness (our sanctification). As believers, we should desire to "put off" the old man of sin and "put on" the new man of righteousness. We should crucify the flesh, feed the spiritual man, and walk in the Spirit (Galatians 5:24, 5:16). We should stop producing the fruit of the flesh (Galatians 5:19-21) and increasingly produce the fruit of the Spirit (Galatians 5:22-23). Perhaps more simply, we need to identify, confess, reduce, and, to the extent possible, eliminate sin in our lives. Why? Because sin is what got us into this mess to begin with, and, more importantly, because God hates sin. He hates it because it is the thing that separates us from having a relationship with Him, something He ordained and desires with His people. As believers, we need to have the same distain for sin that God does. We need to hate it.

In response to the question, "why does God hate sin?", Gotquestions.org comments:

> "God hates sin because it is the very antithesis of His nature... God hates sin because He is Holy... His holiness epitomizes His moral perfection... The Bible presents God's attitude toward sin with strong feelings of hostility, disgust, and utter dislike. For example, sin is described as putrefying sores (Isaiah 1:6), a heavy burden (Psalm 38:4), defiling filth (Titus 1:15; 2 Corinthians 7:1), a binding debt (Matthew 6:12-15), darkness (John 1:6), and a scarlet stain (Isaiah 1:18)".[10]

We have already talked about this, but to have an objective moral law, this law must transcend human definition. It requires belief and accountability to something greater than ourselves. In a general, biblical sense, then, sin is anything that goes against God. This includes rules, laws, statutes, and commandments, but it also encompasses our rebellion and rejection of God in our unbelief and in counterfeit gods that we have created to replace God in our lives. These show up in our addictions, our preoccupation with and worship of money, material things, power, position, health, and other earthly things. Perhaps Galatians 5:19-21 (ESV) puts it best: "Now the works of the flesh are evident: sexual immorality, impurity, sensuality, idolatry, sorcery, enmity, strife, jealousy, fits of anger, rivalries, dissensions, divisions, envy, drunkenness, orgies, and things like these. I warn you, as I warned you before, that those who do such things will not inherit the kingdom of God."

After defining what sin is, I think we can see from the things we have discussed so far that, as Christians, one of our main objectives in our journey to grow in personal holiness should be to reduce and eliminate sin in our lives. So now it's time to try and define some ways to go about doing this.

CHAPTER THIRTEEN

GROWING IN GOD

I have often said that the main benefactor of the Sunday sermon is the pastor who delivers it. Why? Because, normally, he's spent a good part of his week reading, studying, examining, and researching scripture and other biblically based resources in an effort to understand, define, support, and communicate the meaning, purpose, and points of his message. After all that, based on his motivation as a believer, he can't help but grow spiritually. For the congregant to grow, they'd better have listened intently, taken copious notes, written down all the scripture references, taken these notes home, and done a study of their own. This may be somewhat exaggerated, but I think you understand my point.

We must work to grow. We may be unable to put in as much time as the pastor, but it is incumbent on all of us to set aside personal time, daily, to learn and grow in our faith, our relationship with God, and our personal holiness. *Incumbent* means "necessary for someone as a duty or responsibility." What are the things in our lives that we would view in this way? Providing for and protecting our families? Going to work? Attending church? Disciplining our children? There are perhaps only a handful of things that we would deem important enough to include – duties and responsibilities we truly feel are nonnegotiable. Unfortunately, our personal devotion to God may not even make the list.

The "how" of growing in God gives me more consternation and trepidation then anything I have written about so far. My concerns are wrought out of the fact that there are a myriad of ways that we can approach this area of instruction – and the fact that I have a personal bias. The other (perhaps more significant) element is that God will do this differently in all of us. So, my first practical recommendation is to seek God first and foremost; His choice for you should matter the most.

Also, what follows is more academic in nature. Often the best lessons, most effective lessons come from our own experience. It would not be too extreme to say that this is often the only real way we can grow in our relationship with God.

With all that said, I will attempt to offer some things I feel are the most effective ways we can grow in personal holiness and, as a result, in our relationship with the Lord. We have already mentioned a number of factors to keep in mind but let us not forget that the only way we mature and grow in our faith is by remembering that we are both fully responsible and fully dependent.

We must put forth the effort – and then our dependence on the Holy Spirit will do the rest.

A Model for Growing In God

At the risk of being redundant, we have talked about several things that are critical and essential to growing and maturing spiritually: the need to walk in the spirit; realizing our position, power and resources in Christ; the process of growth; our motivation and our commitment; understanding holiness, and our responsibilities and recognition of sin.

These things are all foundational to our understanding, but to benefit from them, we must begin to make them a part of who we are. The result we are looking to achieve is: to grow in a more personal and intimate relationship with God; to increase in personal holiness; to reduce sin in our lives; to walk in and produce the fruit of the spirit; to become a greater witness for Christ; and in all this, ultimately, to bring glory and honor to God.

All areas of discipleship are necessary to achieve these goals, but the pursuit of personal holiness is perhaps the most critical.

Relationships

Most all of what we do in life is based on relationships. (There's one of those "ship" words again, but in this case: the process of developing and becoming "in relation" or in association with others.) We have relationship with our spouse, our children, our family, our coworkers, and our community. As Christians, *relationship* begins first with our faith in Christ and then with others in the church: the body of Christ. As believers, we are commanded to "go and make disciples." This is based on the relationships we form and maintain with others. In the church, we have relationships with people in our congregations, Bible studies, and ministries. These assist in our discipleship, but, as we discussed earlier, they focus more on "disciplines" – the "ministry" and "service"[1] aspects of discipleship as defined in Jerry Bridges' *The Discipline of Grace*.

But what of our growth in personal holiness? What relationships will best facilitate this in our lives? To begin with, the primary relationship we must have and maintain is with God the Holy Spirit. As we have learned, He is ultimately responsible for our spiritual growth. But we also need human relationships. There are at least two main reasons for this: *accountability* and *transparency*. The environment and relationships we choose to grow in have much to do with our success, so let's talk about that next.

We could choose to grow individually alongside the Holy Spirit, but this is really not the best way, nor is it supported by scripture. We are not meant to be loners; we are meant to grow in the fellowship of other believers. Here are some verses that support and encourage that approach:

> "Whoever isolates himself seeks his own desire; he breaks out against all sound judgment." (Proverbs 18:1 ESV)
>
> "Then the Lord God said, "It is not good that the man should be alone..." (Genesis 2:18a ESV)
>
> "Two are better than one, because they have a good reward for their toil." (Ecclesiastes 4:9 ESV)
>
> "And though a man might prevail against one who is alone, two will withstand him—a threefold cord is not quickly broken." (Ecclesiastes 4:12 ESV)
>
> "And let us consider how to stir up one another to love and good works, not neglecting to meet together, as is the habit of some, but encouraging one another, and all the more as you see the Day drawing near." (Hebrews 10:24-25 ESV)
>
> "Bear one another's burdens, and so fulfill the law of Christ." (Galatians 6:2 ESV)
>
> "So Philip ran to him and heard him reading Isaiah the prophet and asked, "Do you understand what you are reading?" And he said, "How can I, unless someone guides me?" And he invited Philip to come up and sit with him." (Acts 8:30-31 ESV)

There are various relationship options we could choose to grow in, but my personal recommendation is that all truly born-again believers should be in at least one one-on-one relationship with another born again believer – if a man, with another man, and if a woman, with another woman. You could opt to go with a group of three or four, or whatever number is considered a manageable small group these days. But if we go that route, I believe we begin to create schedule (commitment) problems and dilute accountability and transparency.

As stated in the introduction, I have been in a number of one-on-one and small group relationships with other men since becoming a believer without really having a foundation or understanding of why they were necessary or important. I have seen firsthand what they have done in my life and the lives of others. We have dealt effectively with the sins of pornography, infidelity, family, marriage and other relationship issues. I have seen firsthand how the Holy Spirit, working through His Word in the accountability and transparency these relationships provide, has brought truth, conviction, repentance, healing, and restoration.

We are all vulnerable to sin, but I truly believe that if this type of relationship is seriously established and committed to, it will help insulate us from the temptations and sin of this world. It will help prevent the "roaring lion" (1 Peter 5:8) from having access to our lives and achieving his evil desires in them. I can't help but believe that the truly born-again believer who has fallen into serious sin would agree with this assessment. There is no silver bullet – if you want to sin badly enough, you will – but if you are truly a Christian, you will agonizingly regret every second of it. When we are in relationships like these, this accountability keeps us strong and helps us avoid the more serious consequences of sin in our lives. This happens not so much because of the physical relationship but because of the spiritual relationship that is emphasized, stressed, realized, and improved between each of us and God.

Accountability and Transparency

The way in which we grow may offer some different alternatives and options, but as already emphasized, the growth itself is not optional. It is commanded by God. If we have committed to a plan to grow and outlined that plan, preferably in writing, the next thing we should discuss is *accountability* and *transparency*.

Accountability and transparency are critical parts of effective and productive personal relationships and should, consequently, help facilitate our desire to grow spiritually. We must have a solid understanding of what these words mean so we can effectively implement them as a part of our plan. Let's first talk about accountability.

Accountability is another one of those words which can be used in a very casual or flippant manner.

We use it without really understanding its full and serious meaning.

Webster defines accountability as "an obligation or willingness to accept responsibility."[2] But the real keys to our understanding are the words *obligation* and *willingness*. *Obligation* is "an act or course of action to which we are morally or legally bound,"[3] and *willingness* is "the quality or state of being prepared to do something."[4] If we have decided to grow in God, are we obligating ourselves to God and are we ready to take action? Are we ready to submit to one another and humble ourselves to follow through?

Accountability relationships do not replace our personal responsibility; their purpose is to help make sure that our responsibilities are executed and achieved. Ultimately, we are accountable to God for our spiritual growth. However, if we are only accountable to ourselves next, there is a good chance that God will hear much repentance and recommitment in our prayers, and many requests for forgiveness. For in many cases, we will tend toward procrastination and not follow through with what we intended to do. I'm sure there are exceptions to this, but without physical accountability, our human nature tends to take over, and we begin to fall short.

If you think about it, almost everything we do in life has some level of accountability to which we are responsible. Work, school, driving a car, building a home, other community activities, civil law – if we are not abiding by the defined rules, laws, or boundaries established in these different areas, we can expect negative consequences. But how do we consider accountability in a personal way with respect to our spiritual growth? I believe this is done by building an accountability relationship with another believer. Leadership Ministries Inc. states:

> "At the heart, accountability is one Christian submitting to the Christ-centered admonition of another Christian in one or more areas of life. Hand in hand with accountability is an attitude of grace and forgiveness, and the taking on of one another's burdens (Romans 12:16, Colossians 3:13, Galatians 6:2). Many men's groups are built around the idea of accountability, but this does not come easily or naturally. True accountability is an element of a mature, long-standing and growing relationship with both God and fellow Christ-followers."[5]

So, at this point, we have discussed why we need accountability and why this accountability needs to be in relationship, or, perhaps better stated, *partnership* with another individual.

What, then, are we looking for in an accountability partner? Someone to monitor our progress and scold us when we fall short? Well, that may be part of it – but let's look more deeply at what this partnership really needs to look like.

To begin with, it's not one-sided accountability but *mutual* accountability that we are looking to develop. We are aiming for an "iron sharpening iron" relationship. We all sin, and we all must humble ourselves to one another if we are going to be successful and fruitful. James 5:16 (ESV) tells us, "Therefore, confess your sins to one another and pray for one another, that you may be healed."

As we can see, humility is key to an accountability relationship. I liked what this user on Gotquestions.org had to say about humility:

> "The Bible describes humility as meekness, lowliness, and absence of self. The Greek word translated "humility" in Colossians 3:12 and elsewhere literally means "lowliness of mind," so we see that humility is a heart attitude, not merely an outward demeanor. One may put on an outward show of humility but still have a heart full of pride and arrogance. Jesus said that those who are "poor in spirit" would have the kingdom of heaven (Matthew 5:3). Being poor in spirit means that only those who admit to an absolute bankruptcy of spiritual worth will inherit eternal life. Therefore, humility is a prerequisite for the Christian…Biblical humility is not only necessary to enter the kingdom, it is

also necessary to be great in the kingdom (Matthew 20:26-27). Here Jesus is our model. Just as He did not come to be served, but to serve, so must we commit ourselves to serving others, considering their interests above our own (Philippians 2:3). This attitude precludes selfish ambition, conceit, and the strife that comes with self-justification and self-defense. Jesus was not ashamed to humble Himself as a servant (John 13:1-16), even to death on the cross (Philippians 2:8). In His humility, He was always obedient to the Father and so should the humble Christian be willing to put aside all selfishness and submit in obedience to God and His Word. True humility produces godliness, contentment, and security."[6]

These words must also be true of one-on-one relationships between believers. We must have an attitude of submission and humility in order to develop an atmosphere of trust and transparency. We must seek out someone we can trust and begin to develop a close and lasting relationship – a person who will challenge and be honest with us, and us with them. One-on-one relationships should not be based on one person being considered over another. What we want in a relationship like this is joint accountability.

In summary, Leadership Ministries, Inc states:

> "An accountability partner is different than a Christian friendship. Not all Christian relationships are accountability relationships. In fact, rarely should they be. When choosing someone to open up to and ask to hold you accountable, it should be someone you trust and respect, with a track record of action and speech reflecting spiritual maturity. Further it should be someone of discretion, who desires to see you grow in your faith, and does not dole out gossip."[7]

Transparency

An important aspect of accountability relationships is *transparency*. This word is defined as "the quality of being done in an open way without secrets" (dictionarycambridge.org)[8]. And from Wikipedia: transparency "is operating in such a way that it is easy for others to see what actions are performed. Transparency implies openness, communication, and *accountability*."[9]

A key aim of an accountability relationship is to identify and kill sin. James 5:16 (ESV), again: "Therefore, confess your sins to one another and pray for one another, that you may be healed." We want to get our sins out of the darkness and into the light so that we can destroy them. To do this in a relationship takes *transparency*. Confessing our sins is half the battle. Once they are in the light, they become exposed, and they lose their power over us. "Take no part in the unfruitful works of darkness, but instead expose them." (Ephesians 5:11 ESV)

There is much more that could be said, but hopefully, what has been discussed provides a good description of the purpose, attitude, and characteristics of an accountability relationship. What takes place in these relationships will vary, but they should include a covenant with God and each other to:

- Meet on a weekly basis
- Openly discuss individual temptation and sin (as trust and transparency grows in the relationship)
- Define areas where Biblical education and understanding is most needed
- Define a plan to study, learn and grow in God's Word
- Pray faithfully and specifically for one another's needs

At this point, (though by no means exhaustively) we have examined many facets of growing in God – the things we need to understand and pursue if we are to continue our journey up Mount Sanctification. This is necessary if we are to mature in our faith, aspire to holiness, and be a useful and effective tool in the hands of God.

Though God may have a very specific and detailed plan for each of our individual lives, we know, for all of us, that this plan includes the responsibility to proclaim the Gospel message and make disciples of all nations, thereby living out our lives as a witness to the truth of God's Word. As we have seen, these things can only be achieved by our devotion to God (our motivation), and our sanctification (the commitment, effort and work to be made holy).

CHAPTER FOURTEEN

MEASURING OUR GROWTH

In order to see how we are doing in all these goals, we will need to measure and evaluate ourselves against biblical standards – what does the Bible lay out as traits which reveal godly character?

Galatians, of course, gives us the nine fruits of the Spirit for this purpose. Once we study and begin to understand these fruits, we can begin to measure ourselves against them to see how we are doing. This will be a very humbling experience. For example, the first fruit of the Spirit is love. We tend to define love more in subjective feelings and emotions. Though an in-depth study is really required to fully grasp its complete meaning, biblical love can be summed up in actions which are giving, sacrificial, and unconditional – in essence, what God did with His Son on the cross to provide reconciliation, justification, atonement, and forgiveness for our sins. So how are we measuring up when we compare our love to a standard like this?

Each of the fruits presents a similar dilemma. When we see what true biblical joy, peace, patience, kindness, goodness, faithfulness, gentleness, and self-control are, we begin to see the challenges that lie before us. The Holy Spirit is our teacher. He is the one who brings the true definition of these fruits to our hearts and lives. It is critical that we re-establish His understanding of them in order to effectively measure our progress and point out where further work is required. Counterfeit fruits abound; we must learn to recognize the real thing. (For a more complete treatment of this subject, see Jerry Bridge's book, *The Fruitful Life*.)[1]

As we put off sin, pursue holiness, and grow and mature more deeply in our relationship with God, we should begin to see a difference in our motivations, desires, and willingness to serve God and people inside and outside the body of Christ. Our study of God's Word, our prayer life, discipleship, and ministry efforts should increase and become more of a priority in our lives. We should be praying and looking for opportunities to be more engaged and more intentional with our faith and the plan that God has for our future. We should be looking for more opportunities to evangelize, witness and share the Gospel with others.

In the end, it is not something that can be quantitatively measured, but only realized by an ongoing change in our lives. We will always fall short, but as Paul admonishes us, "brothers, I do not consider that I have made it my own. But one thing I do:

forgetting what lies behind and straining forward to what lies ahead, I press on toward the goal for the prize of the upward call of God in Christ Jesus." (Philippians 3:13-14 ESV). And also: "Therefore, since we are surrounded by so great a cloud of witnesses, let us also lay aside every weight, and sin which clings so closely, and let us run with endurance the race that is set before us." (Hebrews 12:1 ESV)

> *"Not many of us are living at our best. We linger in the lowlands because we are afraid to climb the mountains. The steepness and ruggedness dismay us, and so we stay in the misty valleys and do not learn the mystery of the hills. We do not know what we lose in our self-indulgence, what glory awaits us if only we had courage for the mountain climb, what blessing we should find if only we would move to the uplands of God." J.R.M*[3]

CHAPTER FIFTEEN

SUMMARY

We have looked at many facets related to understanding the process needed to grow in God. But this book only briefly presents the basic factors that must be considered. It only really introduces the reader to this aspect of Christian duty and responsibility. A continual, ongoing, lifelong study is required. Even then, we can only skim the surface of knowing this God that we serve. "Oh, the depth of the riches and wisdom and knowledge of God! How unsearchable are his judgments and how inscrutable his ways!" (Romans 11:33 ESV)

Again, we must remember that this is not merely an *option* for a true and sincere believer; God commands us to grow, and we must be obedient. Like many other aspects of our faith, we will often fall short, have conflicting and confusing priorities, and fight the ongoing battle between the spirit and the flesh. But this, again, only highlights why our sanctification is so important. As we grow – as we begin to realize the position, resources and power we have in Christ – as we learn how to walk in grace and realize the secure reliable and eternal sovereignty of God – we begin to see the value of this effort and the benefits that are appropriated to us, by the power of the Holy Spirit. We begin to live out the victory that our faith in Christ has secured for us.

When we are saved, our primary motivation in life should change from serving our own interests to loving the Lord our God with all our heart, mind, body, soul, and strength – and then to loving our neighbors as ourselves. To do these things, we must be sanctified by His Word. We must actively pursue holiness, mortify sin, and increase in righteousness. We must make a plan and be dedicated and committed to carrying it out. We must recognize that this as an ongoing and critical aspect of daily living, overcoming the evil of this world, and dealing with our dead sin nature that still clings to us. God gives us the ability and all the resources we need, in Christ, to accomplish this task. Ephesians 1:3-4 (ESV) tells us, "Blessed be the God and Father of our Lord Jesus Christ, who has blessed us in Christ with every spiritual blessing in the heavenly places, even as he chose us in him before the foundation of the world, that we should be holy and blameless before him…"

In closing, these verses from 2 Peter sum up much of what this book has been trying to communicate and what we need to understand and learn:

SUMMARY

"His divine power has granted to us all things that pertain to life and godliness, through the knowledge of him who called us to his own glory and excellence, by which he has granted to us his precious and very great promises, so that through them you may become partakers of the divine nature, having escaped from the corruption that is in the world because of sinful desire. For this very reason, make every effort to supplement your faith with virtue, and virtue with knowledge, and knowledge with self-control, and self-control with steadfastness, and steadfastness with godliness, and godliness with brotherly affection, and brotherly affection with love. For if these qualities are yours and are increasing, they keep you from being ineffective or unfruitful in the knowledge of our Lord Jesus Christ. For whoever lacks these qualities is so nearsighted that he is blind, having forgotten that he was cleansed from his former sins. Therefore, brothers, be all the more diligent to confirm your calling and election, for if you practice these qualities, you will never fall. For in this way there will be richly provided for you an entrance into the eternal kingdom of our Lord and Savior Jesus Christ." (2 Peter 1:3-11 ESV)

EPILOGUE

As I reviewed, applied the final edits, and researched resources for publication of this book, I began to have second thoughts. Was there enough content? Was it big enough to be called a "book"? And more than anything, was it complete? Was it lacking something important that needed to be communicated? I committed this all to prayer and began to wait on the Lord. Over the past several months, He has helped me see several things:

First, this is not my book, it is His. If I keep committing my way to Him, He will be faithful to show me all that needs to be done.

Second, the Bible tells us to, "Be sober-minded; be watchful. Your adversary the devil prowls around like a roaring lion, seeking someone to devour." (1 Peter 5:8 ESV). If you are doing something you feel God has truly called you to, the enemy will want to interfere and attempt to discourage you in anyway possible.

Lastly, during this period, I've had a continuing sense that there was more that needed to be said about our sanctification. Not so much about its definition or process, but in how all-encompassing, and pervasive it should be in our lives. As we have seen, our sanctification is mandated by God and should permeate every aspect of our natural existence. As of late, God has been confirming this repeatedly in various ways. I have seen it more acutely in books I have been reading and studying; in the lessons of our Bible Fellowship Groups; in recent sermons by our Pastor; and in numerous discussions and situations with fellow believers.

The words sanctify, sanctified, and sanctification have been used frequently in this writing to help define, describe and explain the main purpose and process for growing in God. This word can be translated from the Latin, sanctificationem or sanctificare, and means to make holy.[1] In Greek, the word is hagiazo and means hallowed, holy, saint, and sanctify; to set apart for God, to make a person or thing the opposite of common.[2] In Hebrew, the word used is Qadash or Kadesh and means to be consecrated, dedicated or set apart from all else for Yahweh's use.[3]

As we have already seen, it should be the goal of every true Christian to pursue a life of holiness. This is an on-going, ever-growing, and never-ending process. However, I don't think we realize or take as seriously as we should, the overwhelming, all-encompassing nature and expectation of this statement. To one degree or another, we tend to divide or compartmentalize our lives into areas that tend to be mutually exclusive from one another. For example, we may almost always live our lives in view of our family responsibilities and obligations, but do we do this in the higher and more holy relationship we should have with God? Do we make Him a serious part of every aspect of our existence? Unfortunately, if we seriously examined our lives, we would probably see that we only include Him in a half-hearted way or perhaps not at all. In life decisions, we tend to be overly influenced by the world or our own subjective opinion.

One example of this, in the book Counseling, by John MacArthur and The Master's College Faculty, it is evident that the only true road to psychological health is Biblical Counseling and the sanctification of the believer. In the chapter, "The Work of the Spirit and Biblical Counseling", MacArthur writes:

> "Only biblical counseling can offer reliable, authoritative, objective answers. And the objective truth of Scripture is the only tool God uses in the process of sanctification. Jesus prayed Himself, 'Sanctify them in the truth; Thy word is truth' (John 17:17).

Unfortunately, psychology and worldly therapies have usurped the role of sanctification in some Christians thinking. Psychological sanctification has become a substitute for Spirit-filled life. The notion is abroad within the church that psychotherapy is often a more effective change agent—particularly in dealing with the most difficult cases—than the Holy Spirit who sanctifies.

But can psychotherapy possibly accomplish something that the Holy Spirit cannot? Can an earthly therapist achieve more than a heavenly Comforter? Is behavior modification more helpful than sanctification?"[4]

John answers these questions quite succinctly, "Of course not".[5] How often in our lives do we, as Christians, pursue a worldly, secular solution or opinion rather than seeking the answers to life issues as a continuing part of our sanctification in God's Word? We are too often ready and conditioned to seek the worlds way.

The book, Ordering Your Private World, offers another example of the effects of neglected sanctification. The author, Gordon MacDonald, in his early adult years, had risen quickly to become a prominent Pastor of a midsized church that was growing, active and vibrant. He had become

EPILOGUE

increasingly immersed in the day-to-day business of running the church, and had lost touch, not only with God, but with his family and the real needs of his church body.

One day, he hit the proverbial *"wall"*, and was confronted with the reality of what he had become. As he states in the preface, "Natural gifts such as personal charisma, mental brightness, emotional strength, and organizational ability can impress and motivate people for a long time. Sometimes they can be mistaken for spiritual vitality and depth. Sadly, we do not have a Christian culture that easily discriminates between a person of spiritual depth and a person of raw talent...The result is that more than a few people can be fooled into thinking they are being influenced by a spiritual giant when, in fact, they are being manipulated by a (*spiritual*) dwarf."[6]

MacDonald goes on to summarize the cause of his dilemma when he felt God speaking to his heart; *"Now you know what it's like to live out of an empty soul."*[7] He goes on to state that an empty soul—*"is empty when one tries to do soul-based things but makes little or no effort to keep that soul filled."*[8]

The book is a very worthwhile read, especially for those who find themselves caught up in a similar situation, but there is much here for all of us to learn. I don't believe MacDonald ever actually uses the word *"sanctification"* to describe his need, but I believe this was what he had been lacking. Without this, we all tend to cordon off a world of our own making, of our own thoughts and priorities. A world that can quickly become self-centered and godless, fooling both ourselves and those around us. As MacDonald did, we must transform it, so it becomes a haven for a true, deep and full relationship with our creator. Only then will we be prepared to handle what life and God throw at us, and not by our power, but by His.

Shepherding a Child's Heart, by Tedd Tripp, is another book that helped me realize how all-encompassing the pursuit of holiness should be in the life of a believer. It was written to help parents understand and learn how to raise their children Biblically.

As Tripp points out in the Preface, "Parents tend to focus on the externals of behavior rather than the internal overflow of the heart."[9] We end up focusing on the *what* of behavior as opposed to the *why*. Tripp goes on to explain that when we do this "we miss the heart".[10] We miss the heart in three ways:
1. "We miss the subtle idols of the heart"
2. "We miss the gospel", and
3. "We miss the glory of God"[11]

In the overall picture, we miss the opportunity to enhance or begin the process of sanctification, in both our children, our spouse, and ourselves.

In teaching the book many times, Tripp found a common reaction and response was, "These truths you are teaching are not just about our children; they are about me".[12] I can personalize that response. When I agreed to read and study this book with a new parent, I quickly realized that the truths in this book were vitally important to my own spiritual growth.

Overall, this book really provides a great basis for the sanctification of the whole family and in other relationships as well. In life it is the heart of the issue we need to get to, and this is too often ignored.

Though there are many others, the last book I would like to mention in this chapter, is "The Holiest of All", by Andrew Murray.

Murray opens his book by acknowledging the problem he sees in the growth and maturity of those who claim Christ as savior and Lord in their lives.

In the preface and introduction to the book, Murray is clear about his concern for those who would call themselves Christians. He sees what he calls "the lack of wholeheartedness, of steadfastness, of perseverance, and of progression in the Christian life."[13] Many seem at a standstill, which brings doubt about their true conversion, while others have backslidden into "a life of worldliness, formality, and indulgence."[14]

For those that are true believers, he offers the study of the epistle of Hebrews as a way out of their predicament stating that, "The knowledge of Christ Jesus that we need for conversion does not suffice for growth, for progress, for sanctification, and for maturity."[15] and that "the great objective of the epistle (Hebrews) is to show us that if we only follow the Lord fully and yield ourselves wholly to what God, in Christ, is ready to do, we will find, in the Gospel and in Christ, everything we need for a life of joy, strength, and final victory."[16] This is victory that we can realize in our day to day walk with Christ. It is the victory that only comes and is revealed through the ongoing process of our sanctification.

You can spend much time and energy in the beginning chapters of Hebrews (esp. ch. 1-6) in trying to determine or understand the spiritual condition of those to which the epistle is written. It is clear they have embraced the Gospel of Christ, but are they truly "born again" believers? The study can get even more confusing if you consider the idea or possibility of gaining and then loosing your salvation (Hebrews 6:4-6). In a recent sermon series by our Pastor, these issues were very clearly and adequately addressed. However, throughout the sermon, I kept pondering the thought that no one can really know another person's spiritual condition. We may guess at it based on a person's life and works (see chapter 3) but only God really knows. It was than, it seemed to me, that the author was more than likely fully aware of this and that the primary teaching and encouragement in these passages were first, to encourage the sanctification of the true believer, and/or, secondly, to evangelize those that were not.

In essence then, these chapters, and perhaps the whole book of Hebrews, was written to emphasize,

EPILOGUE

encourage, teach, and stress the all important and all encompassing role of sanctification in a believers life.

As the people in my Bible Fellowship Group can testify, I have mentioned this many times in our Sunday meetings. So often the studying we participate in, the subjects discussed, and the questions raised, seem always to point to this need and concern.

In closing, I would like to conclude with a page out of "God's Best Secrets, The Secret of Fellowship" by Andrew Murray.

FROM DAY TO DAY
"The inward man is being renewed day by day."
2 Corinthians 4:16

> "There is one lesson that all young christians should learn, and that is the absolute necessity of fellowship with Jesus every day. This lesson is not always taught at the beginning of the Christian life, nor is it always understood by the young convert. He should realize that the grace he has received—the forgiveness of his sins, his acceptance as God's child, his joy in the Holy Spirit—can only be preserved by daily renewal in fellowship with Jesus Christ Himself.
>
> Many Christians backslide because this truth is not clearly taught. They are unable to stand against the temptations of the world and of their

old nature. They strive to do their best to fight against sin and to serve God, but they have no strength.

Read Matthew 11:25-30. Christ says, "Come to me...and I will give you rest...Learn from me...and you will find rest for your souls" (vv. 28-29). The Lord will teach us just how meek and humble He is. Bow before Him, tell Him that you long for Him and His love, and He will let His love rest on you. This is a thought not only for young Christians, but also for those who love the Lord.

If you desire to live this life of fellowship with Christ, if you wish to enjoy this blessed experience each day, then learn the lesson of spending time each day, without exception, in the fellowship with your Lord. In this way, your inner man will be renewed from day to day."[17]

GROWING IN GOD

ESSENTIAL / RECOMMENDED STUDY MATERIALS

1. John MacArthur, online sermon (Grace to You – gty.org), "The Fullness of God"
2. Am I Really Saved, John MacArthur, online article (Grace to You – gty.org), "Examine Yourself"
3. Jerry Bridges, *The Fruitful Life* (Colorado Springs, CO: NavPress, 2006)
4. J.I. Packer, *Knowing God*, (Downers Grove, IL: InterVarsity Press 1993)
5. John MacArthur, "The Essential Work of the Holy Spirit," online sermon series (Grace To You – gty.org)
6. John MacArthur, "Our Resources in Christ," online sermon series (Grace To You – gty.org)
7. Jerry Bridges, *The Disciplines of Grace* (Colorado Springs, CO: NavPress 2006)
8. Jerry Bridges, *The Pursuit of Holiness*, (Colorado Springs, CO: NavPress 2006)
9. Gordon MacDonald, *Ordering Your Private World* (Nashville, TN:W Publishing Group an Imprint of Thomas Nelson 2017)

10. Andrew Murray, *The Holiest Of All* (New Kensington, PA:Whitaker House 2004)
11. John MacArthur, "Sanctification: The Believers Transformation", online sermon series, (Grace To You – gty.org)
12. John MacArthur, "Sanctification: The Believers Transformation pt. 2", online sermon series, (Grace To You – gty.org)
13. John MacArthur, "Sanctification: The Honorable Obsession", online sermon series, (Grace To You – gty.org)

NOTES

PREFACE

1. Lee Strobel, *The Case For Christ*, (Grand Rapids, MI: Zondervan 1998)

CHAPTER TWO – Affirming Your Faith

1. Charles Haddon Spurgeon, online sermon (The Spurgeon Center – spurgeon.org), "Why Are Men Saved," paragraph 3.
2. Charles Haddon Spurgeon, online sermon (The Spurgeon Center – spurgeon.org), "Why Are Men Saved," paragraph 3.
3. John MacArthur, online sermon (Grace to You - gty.org), "The Fullness of God, Part 2," paragraph 21.

CHAPTER THREE – Am I Really Saved?

1. John MacArthur, online article (Grace to You – gty.org), "Examine Yourself," pages 1-3
2. MacArthur, 1
3. MacArthur, 2
4. MacArthur, 2
5. MacArthur, 2
6. MacArthur, 2
7. MacArthur, 2

8. MacArthur, 2
9. MacArthur, 3
10. Encyclopedia.com, online definition of *repent*.
11. Jerry Bridges, *The Fruitful Life* (Colorado Springs, CO: NavPress, 2006)
12. MacArthur, 3
13. Bible Study Fellowship Tract, "Steps to Assurance" (San Antonio TX: BSF International), 5

CHAPTER SIX – The Trinity – Father, Son, and Holy Spirit

1. Don Stewart, "What Does the Hebrew Term Elohim Mean?" online article, (blueletterbible.org)
2. J.I. Packer, *Knowing God*, (Downers Grove, IL: InterVarsity Press 1993), 69
3. John MacArthur, "The Essential Work of the Holy Spirit," online sermon series (Grace To You – gty.org), paragraph 14
4. J.I. Packer, 68
5. Charles Stanley, "The Truth About the Trinity," online article, (In Touch Ministries, crosswalk.com), paragraph 2

CHAPTER SEVEN – Walk in the Spirit

1. John MacArthur, "Our Resources in Christ," online sermon series (Grace To You – gty.org)

2.   John MacArthur, "The Fullness of God," on-line sermon series (Grace To You – gty.org)

CHAPTER EIGHT – Keys to Walking in the Spirit

1.   Jerry Bridges, *The Fruitful Life* (Colorado Springs, CO: NavPress 2006), 79-80
2.   Jerry Bridges, 17
3.   Jerry Bridges, 17
4.   Jerry Bridges, quoting Dutch reformed pastor George W. Bethune, 18

CHAPTER NINE – Motivation and Commitment

1.   Dictionary, *motivation*, online definition, Google search
2.   positivepsychology.com, *motivation*, online definition
3.   Jerry Bridges, *The Fruitful Life* (Colorado Springs, CO: NavPress 2006), 12
4.   Jerry Bridges, 13
5.   Jerry Bridges, 14
6.   Jerry Bridges, 15
7.   Dictionary, *commitment*, on-line definition, Google search
8.   Jerry Bridges, *The Disciplines of Grace* (Colorado Springs, CO: NavPress 2006), 12

CHAPTER TEN – Discipleship

1. Serenity Carr (Asst. Editor), learnersdictionary.org, paraphrase
2. Jerry Bridges, *The Discipline of Grace* (Colorado Springs, CO: NavPress 2006), 20
3. Got Questions, "What is sanctification?" gotquestions.org, paragraph 2

CHAPTER ELEVEN – Holiness

1. R. C. Sproul, "The Meaning of Holiness," online sermon series (Ligonier.org), paragraph 18
2. R. C. Sproul, paragraph 3-4
3. R. C. Sproul, paragraph 14
4. Jerry Bridges, *The Pursuit of Holiness*, (Colorado Springs, CO: NavPress 2006), 3

CHAPTER TWELVE – Sin

1. Dictionary, *sin*, on-line definition, lexico.com/en/definition/sin
2. Jerry Bridges, *The Disciplines of Grace* (Colorado Springs, CO: NavPress 2006), 36
3. Jerry Bridges, 36-37
4. Dictionary.com, definition of *dispise*
5. Jerry Bridges, 36-37
6. Jerry Bridges, 37
7. Jerry Bridges, 37

8. Dictionary.com, definition of *indictment*, on-line definition
9. Got Questions "Why God Hates Sin?" gotquestions.org, paragraph 1
10. Got Questions, paragraph 2

CHAPTER THIRTEEN – Growing in God

1. Jerry Bridges, *The Disciplines of Grace*, (Colorado Springs, CO: NavPress 2006), 20
2. Webster online dictionary, *accountability*, merriam-webster.com
3. Dictionary, *obligation*, online definition, Google search
4. Dictionary, *willingness*, on-line definition, Google search
5. Leadership Ministries Inc., *accountability*, leadmin.org, paragraph 3
6. Got Questions, *humility*, got questions.org, paragraph 1 and 3
7. Leadership Ministries Inc., paragraph 4
8. Dictionarycambridge.org, *transparency*, online definition
9. Wikipedia, *transparency*, online definition

CHAPTER FOURTEEN – Measuring Our Growth

1. Jerry Bridges, *The Fruitful Life*, (Colorado Springs, CO:NavPress 2006)

2. Mrs. Charles E. Cowman, *Streams in The Desert Vol I* (Grand Rapids MI: Zondervan 1965), 3 (Jan. 2)

EPILOGUE

1. Etymonline.com, sanctification, online definition of word in Latin
2. Greekwordstudies.blogspot.com, sanctification, online definition of word in Greek
3. En.wiki books.org, *sanctification*, online definition of word in Hebrew
4. John MacArthur and The Masters College Faculty, *Counseling* (Nashville, TN:Thomas Nelson 2005), 80
5. John MacArthur and The Masters College Faculty, 80
6. Gordon MacDonald, *Ordering Your Private World* (Nashville, TN:W Publishing Group an Imprint of Thomas Nelson 2017), xvii-xviii
7. Gordon MacDonald, xviii
8. Gordon MacDonald, xviii
9. Tedd Tripp, *Shepherding a Child's Heart* (Wapwallopen, PA:Shepherd Press 2005), xi
10. Tedd Tripp, xi
11. Tedd Tripp, xi-xii
12. Tedd Tripp, xii
13. Andrew Murray, *The Holiest Of All* (New Kensington, PA:Whitaker House 2004), 5
14. Andrew Murray, 5

NOTES

15. Andrew Murray, 5
16. Andrew Murray, 6
17. Andrew Murray, *God's Best Secrets* (New Kensington, PA:Whitaker House 1998), 13

Made in United States
Orlando, FL
21 March 2023